SENSORY PROCESSING 101

by
**Dayna Abraham,
Claire Heffron,
Pamela Braley, and
Lauren Drobnjak**

Sensory Processing 101 Endorsements

What a practical, reassuring, visually appealing, lovely book! Not just an excellent introductory "101" course on SPD, this is also an "All-in-One" resource book, with its engaging activities and reproducible review pages to slip in your pocket or share with others who care for children with sensory challenges.

— **CAROL STOCK KRANOWITZ,** AUTHOR, *THE OUT-OF-SYNC CHILD*

I am really excited about this book because I know it is going to help parents like me. As a mom of three boys, our family has dealt with our share of sensory processing issues. Even though I am a Physical Therapist, I didn't initially identify the cause of the problem which lead to frustration and tantrums. Once we knew what it was and what to do, everything changed for the better.

— **HOLLY HOMER, MPT,** FOUNDER OF KIDS ACTIVITIES BLOG AND CO-AUTHOR OF 101 KIDS ACTIVITIES THAT ARE THE BESTEST, FUNNEST EVER!

As a classroom teacher for more than 20 years, this book has given me tremendous insight into working with students who are easily overstimulated by noise, and struggle to sit still and pay attention. The strategies suggested in this book and the explanations given make so much sense! I feel like sensory processing is piece of the puzzle that has been missing my entire career. Now I can finally put everything together to help teachers and children in the classroom.

— **VANESSA LEVIN,** FOUNDER OF PRE-KPAGES.COM AND AUTHOR OF *A FABULOUS FIRST YEAR AND BEYOND*

This reader-friendly book is a handy guide for parents that have children with sensory issues of any kind. With great gentleness and humility, Sensory Processing 101 describes sensory processing disorder from both a therapist's perspective and a parent's perspective - unveiling and simplifying sensory issues from an intolerance of getting messy to having to put anything and everything in the mouth. Grounded in clinical expertise and loaded with personal experiences, this book is a gem for parents looking for answers.

— **ANGELA HANSCOM, MOT, OTR/L,** CEO AND FOUNDER OF TIMBERNOOK AND AUTHOR OF *BALANCED & BAREFOOT*

ISBN 978-0-692-51836-6

First Printing, 2015

Ordering Information:
www.sensoryprocessing101.com

—

Designed by Kristian Bjornard
www.ookb.co

Disclaimer: The activities in this book are intended for sensory play and exploration. These activities are not a replacement for therapy to address Sensory Processing Disorder in children. However, some activities may be appropriate for children who have sensory needs with the supervision and recommendation of an occupational therapist. All activities should be facilitated and supervised by an adult. Some of the activities in this book may not be appropriate for children who have allergies or sensitivities to certain sensory materials or foods used for sensory play.

CONTENTS

PART 2: SENSORY ACTIVITIES FOR KIDS

PART 3: SENSORY RESOURCES

How to Use This Book

It could be that you picked up this book because you have a child who becomes overstimulated and can't seem to control himself in a noisy, active setting like a birthday party. Maybe you have a child in your classroom who has a tantrum any time she gets glue, paint, or marker on her hands. Does your child have a hard time keeping things out of his mouth, chewing on everything from his shirt to his pencil to his fingernails? This book will help you determine the real reason behind some of these behaviors.

Whether you are a parent, educator, caregiver, or therapist, you will learn about each sensory system and how it contributes to healthy child development. In addition, you will find several helpful suggestions, tips, and activities you can try at home or in the classroom.

Supporting healthy sensory processing is an important part of promoting overall health in every child. Therefore, the information in this book pertains to all children regardless of whether they have Sensory Processing Disorder (SPD) diagnoses.

For more information and resources about sensory processing, visit Lemon Lime Adventures at *lemonlimeadventures.com* and The Inspired Treehouse at *theinspiredtreehouse.com*.

WHO IS THIS BOOK FOR?

Sensory Processing 101 gives you an easy-to-read overview of the body's sensory systems and how these systems work together as well as practical suggestions for how you can best support sensory development in children.

- **Parents and caregivers:** This book will help you understand the role sensory processing plays in your child's development. If your child exhibits behaviors that may be related to sensory needs such as biting, constantly making noise, or seeking out movement, the resources and activities in this book will help you address those behaviors.

- **Teachers:** This book explains how the sensory systems contribute to every student's ability to learn and function in the classroom. The resources in this book will help you better understand and support the students who can't seem to sit still, can't stop making noise, or can't pay attention and follow directions. You will also learn to identify certain behaviors as red flags for possible sensory processing concerns.

- **Therapists:** Use this book to select activities to use during therapy sessions or to recommend activities that families can try at home so you can meet the specific sensory needs of your clients. This book also contains several reproducible resources for you to share with parents, caregivers, and teachers. Finally, this book will give you a closer look at sensory processing from a parent and teacher's point of view, which will help you better understand how your interventions impact families and teachers.

Disclaimer: The activities in this book are intended for sensory play and exploration. These activities are not a replacement for therapy to address Sensory Processing Disorder in children. However, some activities may be appropriate for children who have sensory needs with the supervision and recommendation of an occupational therapist. All activities should be facilitated and supervised by an adult. Some of the activities in this book may not be appropriate for children who have allergies or sensitivities to certain sensory materials or foods used for sensory play.

HOW TO USE EACH SECTION

This book contains three books in one:

· **Sensory Processing Explained** – This section provides a breakdown of each sensory system from a therapist's point of view and from the perspective of a parent and educator. If you have an interest in a specific sensory system, you can focus on that system's section. Alternatively, you can read all the sections to gain a better understanding of how the systems work together. This part of the book is similar to a conversation in that it provides a well-rounded view of sensory processing: what it looks like when all the senses are functioning properly and what it looks like when one or more of the systems have a problem. In this section, you will also find common red flags for sensory processing problems and advice for when and how to get help.

· **Sensory Activities for Kids** – In this section, you will find our favorite sensory activities for kids. You can include these activities in everyday play with kids at home or at school to support the development of children's sensory systems. This section also includes tips for how to modify the activities based on children's sensory preferences. Some activities are quick and simple, while others require planning ahead to use at a play date, in the classroom, or in a therapy group.

· **Sensory Resources** – This section contains helpful websites related to sensory processing, suggestions for support groups for parents and caregivers of children who have sensory needs, cheat sheets with quick overviews of each sensory system, and other useful printable resources. You are welcome to print or copy the reproducible pages in this section and share them with others. For example, a parent could print them and provide them to a teacher or caregiver who is working with their child for the first time. A therapist might copy pages to share with teachers or parents to inform them about a child's sensory needs. The checklist of red flag behaviors was designed by a pediatric occupational therapist. Parents can use this checklist to document concerns about their child's behaviors for a pediatrician or therapist. Therapists can use the checklist as a quick screening to indicate sensory processing concerns during classroom, home, or clinic observations. This is your go-to section for finding information to share with others or to find quick, easy-to-read overviews about sensory processing.

Finally, this book also includes an index organized according to common behaviors that may be associated with sensory concerns. Use the index to locate information and activities that correspond to the specific behaviors you observe in a child.

A Note From the Authors

FROM DAYNA AT LEMON LIME ADVENTURES

Sensory processing disorder can be a confusing and overwhelming diagnosis for a parent or educator to handle. I still have to pause for a moment when I'm asked to describe my son's struggles. I have landed on the phrase, "He struggles with sensory integration." But I'm never sure if it adequately describes my son's issues.

What I do know is that my son's struggles opened the door for me to spread awareness, find resources, and build a community to support others who are in the same boat.

I am not a therapist or a doctor.

I am a mom raising a child who has sensory needs.

I am an educator who taught in the early childhood field for 12 years.

I am simply just like you.

I will attempt to explain sensory processing from my perspective. I will not attempt to use medical terms, explain what I don't understand myself, or pretend to be an expert. My goal is to give you hope, share what I have learned, and hopefully help you understand your child more deeply.

FROM THE TEAM AT THE INSPIRED TREEHOUSE

In our pediatric therapy practice, we see many kids who struggle with sensory processing issues that impact their ability to function independently and successfully at school, at home, and in their communities.

However, we see many more children who are otherwise typically functioning, but they exhibit behavior problems, attention problems, and motor delays. Some of these issues may be due to a lack of exposure to active play experiences that were a common part of childhood years ago.

We do not want any child to be left behind simply because they have not had these developmental experiences. That's why our mission at The Inspired Treehouse is to provide easy-to-read information about child development and to design simple activities that promote a wide range of developmental skills in children.

We wrote this book from the perspective of pediatric therapists. But we are moms too, so everything we write is near and dear to our hearts as we watch our own children learn and grow.

SENSORY PROCESSING EXPLAINED

CHAPTER 1

Sensory Processing and Sensory Processing Disorder - An Overview

What Is Sensory Processing?
A Therapist's Perspective

Getting messy is a wonderful play experience for young children, and we recommend it. But sensory integration is more complicated than just getting your hands dirty.

Here's a quick glimpse into what sensory processing means.

A child's sensory systems pick up information from the child's surroundings and send that information to the nervous system, which processes the information and generates a response or reaction to what is happening around him.

The sensory systems include:
· The auditory system – the sense of hearing
· The olfactory system – the sense of smell
· The oral sensory system – the sense of taste
· The vestibular system – how we sense where our bodies in space
· The proprioceptive system – our sense of the way our bodies move
· The tactile system – the sense of touch
· The visual systems – the sense of sight
· The interoceptive system, which is responsible for the general sense of our body's physical condition, such as hunger, thirst, and internal discomfort.

Sensory experiences are so powerful they can "rewire" the brain.

These experiences can help children understand their environments more clearly, making them feel safe. Or the experiences can be overwhelming, causing children to become defensive and withdrawn.

> **Sensory experiences are so powerful they can "rewire" the brain.**

In addition, no two children will ever respond to a sensory experience in exactly the same way. For example, if you offer putty to two children, one child may squeeze it tightly and let it run through her fingers, enjoying how it feels cool and mushy. The other child may drop it immediately, irritated by the same sensation.

This is sensory processing: the way the body receives, analyzes, and responds to the signals it receives from its environment. Thoughtful, guided exposure to playful sensory experiences is the best way to promote healthy development of the sensory systems. This ensures that little bodies learn to process, integrate, and generate appropriate responses to the sensory information in their environments.

Sometimes children experience difficulty with processing or tolerating one or more types of sensory input. Several possible medical reasons can cause this difficulty, but one of the most common is Sensory Processing Disorder (SPD). For children with SPD, their bodies do not organize and integrate sensory information properly, which makes it difficult for those children to generate appropriate responses to their environments. This can result in a wide range of confusing and sometimes negative behaviors. When children demonstrate significant sensory processing concerns, exposure to everyday sensory play experiences may not be enough to manage their behaviors and to treat the underlying cause of these behaviors. These children may require assessment and intervention designed by an occupational therapist or other medical professional.

Sensory Processing Disorder
A Parent and Educator's Point of View

Sensory Processing Disorder can be a confusing term. No two children are alike, and no two cases are the same. Doctors and researchers are still figuring out the details of the sensory systems, which makes the issue difficult to understand. As a parent and an educator, I have heard a wide range of terminology referring to sensory processing:

Sensory, Sensory Integration, Sensory Needs, Sensory Overload, Sensory Seeking

To add to the confusion, you might find another word attached to one of the terms listed above:

Disorder, Dysfunction

One of the most important things I learned is that sensory needs run across a spectrum similar to the colors of a rainbow. Children can be over-stimulated by the world around them, or they can be unresponsive to their surroundings, which causes them to seek additional input, usually in a socially unacceptable manner. Children can be a little of both, fall somewhere in the middle, be exclusively on one end of the spectrum, or exhibit problems in only one area. That is what makes "sensory processing" so complicated and confusing.

As a parent, I see my fun, smart child turn into someone I don't know or understand in the blink of an eye. I hear him cry because his socks "don't like his feet." I endure yelling, screaming, and tantrums because something doesn't go as planned. I often compare my son to a house of cards: meticulous and intriguing but also delicate and complex.

As an educator in the classroom, I watched as a child with sensory needs ran himself into walls. I witnessed parents at their wit's end because of their child's need to put everything in his mouth. I taught lessons with children bouncing on balls to stay focused. I comforted many children as they cowered under a desk because the noise of the classroom was too much for them to handle.

As a parent, I was frustrated and didn't know where to start. As an educator, I was confused because I was never trained in this area of child development. So I asked the questions, "What is wrong here? How can I help? What can I do?"

Over the last five years, I read, asked questions, found some answers, and most importantly, found support. The last section of this book contains some of the support groups, books, and websites we found useful in our quest to learn more about sensory processing. Our hope is that you will find answers to your questions, ideas for activities, and a support system to help you as you learn to meet your child's sensory needs.

5 Common Sensory Processing Myths: Busted

If you look around the web, you'll find thousands of articles, blog posts, and opinions about sensory processing. Some are amazing resources for parents, teachers, and therapists. However, you can also find a lot of misleading information – not to mention the information that is downright false. Let's debunk some of the most common myths and misconceptions you might hear about sensory processing.

MYTH 1: SENSORY MEANS GETTING YOUR HANDS MESSY.

TRUTH: Kids experience the world using their entire bodies. When you're planning sensory play experiences, remember to get the whole body involved. Don't get stuck on activities that appeal only to the hands.

Expose your child to play experiences that engage all senses: hearing, sight, taste, smell, movement, and touch. For example, bowling with a light plastic bowling ball is a different sensory experience than bowling with a heavy weighted exercise ball. Instead of just asking your child to carry a ball with his hands, ask if he can carry it between his knees or elbows. This type of play will allow your child to explore how his body moves in space and how it works against resistance. Draw attention to sensory experiences during everyday life and play. For example, can your child hear her rice cereal pop when you pour the milk? Can she see baking soda fizz when you add vinegar?

The goal is to form a healthy integration among all sensory systems so children can listen, attend, develop strong coordinated bodies, stay curious, initiate interactions, and remain calm and focused in their environments.

MYTH 2: SENSORY ACTIVITIES ARE EASY. YOU JUST SET THEM UP, AND THE KIDS WILL KNOW WHAT TO DO.

TRUTH: It is important for children to explore their environments independently to promote creativity and independent thinking. However, guided sensory play has benefits, too. Ask yourself if you want the activity to have a specific purpose, such as to learn a motor skill, to learn to tolerate the feel of a texture, or to engage and attend for a certain length of time. Or is the purpose of the activity simply to have fun?

When children encounter a sensory experience, it can be a wonderful opportunity to expose and build their sensory systems through different avenues of play. Model and demonstrate ways to play and interact with the materials you present to the child. One way to do this is through pretend play. Structure the activity so it has a purpose, such as building something, finding an object, moving materials from one place to another, and so on. Siblings and friends make great models, too. Presenting unfamiliar activities in a group setting can bolster feelings of security and confidence and allows for greater interaction and expansion of play.

MYTH 3: ALL SENSORY ACTIVITIES ARE BENEFICIAL FOR ALL KIDS.

TRUTH: All children are wired differently and will respond in their own unique way to the sensory experiences presented to them. Observe your child during everyday routines, and design sensory activities that meet his or her needs.

For example:

· *Does she like to touch everything?* Build sensory bins into the play routine.
· *Is he extremely sensitive to certain noises?* Gradually introduce a variety of non-threatening new sounds through toys and listening games.
· *Does she get excitable and have trouble calming down?* Think about adding some calming sensory input – such as deep pressure, low lighting, or soft sounds.

Sensory integration is all about the individual child and what he or she needs in the moment.

See the *Sensory Activities* and *Sensory Resources* sections of this book for more ideas for sensory play.

MYTH 4: IF A CHILD IS CAUTIOUS ABOUT PARTICIPATING IN A SENSORY EXPERIENCE, MAKE HIM JUMP IN AND GIVE IT A GO. HE'LL LIKE IT ONCE HE TRIES IT.

TRUTH: When a child is cautious about sensory play, he or she usually has a good reason.

Allow children to approach activities on their own without forcing it upon them. Let them watch first. Then, gradually adapt the activity to meet their needs. Slowly move from passive observation toward more active interaction with the sensory activity. For example, if a child is reluctant to touch playdough, suggest he use utensils to cut and flatten it before touching it with his hands.

Think of ways to make the activity less intense if the child is reluctant or more intense when the child is ready for a richer sensory experience.

· *Do you have a child who cannot tolerate finger paint?* Use a paintbrush first.
· *Still too much?* Suggest he hold your hand while you paint the picture, or let him observe you interacting with the paints.

· *What about a child who is super excited when he sees the finger paints?* Take it to another level. For example, let him paint with his feet. Or add a texture, such as sand, to the finger paints.

Model sensory activities for your child. Let her see someone she loves and trusts engaging and having fun with sensory play. Let her watch and keep the experience open for her to join in when she is ready. Keep in mind that the end goal of sensory activities is for children to have a strong, stable, and healthy sense of themselves in their environment.

MYTH 5: MORE SENSORY INPUT IS ALWAYS BETTER.

TRUTH: Exposure to a variety of sensory experiences does support healthy development in children, but you can overdo it. Remember to keep it simple. Try not to overwhelm children by doing too much at once. Introduce sensory play gradually, one sensation at a time, and watch your child's responses and behavior. If he is enjoying himself, build on that and expose him to more.

For example, fill a plastic tub with rice and allow your child to run her hands through the rice, exploring the texture and feel.

· *Does she enjoy it?* Does it keep her attention? Next time, add a visual component by tossing in some objects for your child to find.
· *What about incorporating a song or a rhyme that asks her to find a specific object for auditory input?* As one example, sing Old MacDonald. The child can then find the animals you hid in the rice as you mention each one in the song.

Subtle, gradual exposure is the key to successful sensory play.

CHAPTER 2

The Auditory System

A Therapist's Perspective

The auditory sense is how we receive and process the information from the sensory organs inside our ears. When we hear a sound, it travels to our brains to be analyzed so we can generate a response. What should we do next? What is going on around us? Is the sound alerting us to something dangerous or important, like a fire alarm or a honking car horn? Is the sound quiet and calming, like classical music or the whirring of a fan?

The inner ear has two important organs that work as partners to fulfill big jobs. In general, the cochlea translates and interprets every sound we hear (what is it?), and the vestibule helps move the sound along to the brain to generate a response to the sound (what should I do next?). The inner ear and the sense of hearing also contribute to our vestibular system, helping us with movement and balance.

A HEALTHY AUDITORY SYSTEM

Children with healthy auditory systems can respond to sounds naturally, looking when you call their names or turning their heads toward a sound. They can follow verbal directions from their teacher or parent. A child with

a functioning auditory system from a sensory perspective can filter out sounds that are not important, such as a friend tapping his pencil on the neighboring desk, while tuning into sounds that are important, such as the teacher's direction to start working on an assignment or his mom calling him for dinner over the television.

Most children function in noisy environments without missing a beat. Common sounds neither distract nor overwhelm these children, and they often react automatically, knowing just what to do when they hear familiar noises like the school bell or the alarm clock. Children typically enjoy toys and play activities that appeal to the auditory system, and they gravitate toward toys that make noise or activities that go along with a song.

Children with healthy auditory systems have good awareness of their environment, develop motor planning abilities to respond appropriately to sounds, and generate protective responses to dangerous situations. A fully functioning auditory system is also integral for the development of listening skills, communication, and social skills.

PROBLEMS WITH THE AUDITORY SYSTEM

Difficulties arise when the brain does not accurately interpret and respond to auditory information. Children's brains help them listen, process what they hear, and understand what has been said. Some children misinterpret information they hear or miss subtle information such as a single word. For example, the verbal direction, "Line up for recess" is quite different from, "Line up behind Tommy for recess." If children miss one small part of a direction, it can alter their response entirely.

Two more common examples of difficulties with the auditory system are hypersensitivity and hyposensitivity to sound.

Children who are hypersensitive to auditory input are overwhelmed and even frightened by the volume, pitch, and unpredictability of common environmental sounds. These children may:

- Attempt to avoid and withdraw from noisy, crowded environments
- Startle easily or appear very distracted because they focus on every noise around them
- Appear agitated and always ready to flee
- Show physical signs of avoidance of sound, such as covering their ears or ducking their heads

The opposite extreme are children who are hyposensitive to sound. Hyposensitive children do not register important auditory cues in their environments. These children may:

· Appear as though they do not hear the sounds around them
· Fail to generate appropriate motor responses to auditory input, such as following directions, turning to look when you call their names, looking in the direction of a loud noise, and so on
· Be noisy and seem to be always talking, singing, humming, and making sounds to generate additional auditory input for themselves
· Talk out loud while performing a task, prompting themselves as they complete each step
· Fail to respond when you speak to them because they simply do not know you are talking to them
· Have difficulty remembering what you told them

Hearing and responding to environmental sounds is only one aspect of the auditory system. Auditory processing is an even more complex layer of the auditory system. Auditory processing refers to the ability to discriminate between similar sounds and to understand information presented verbally.

A Parent and Educator's Point of View

The auditory system seems like it should be simple enough to explain. We all grew up learning about our sense of hearing. You either hear or you don't, right? What most people do not learn about is the important role this system plays in our body's ability to feel in control and to feel centered. The auditory system continues to baffle me, especially as it relates to my own son. This system is not simply about our ability to hear but also our ability to listen.

> **Footsteps, the sound of the wind against your ears, a door creaking, a flushing toilet, even the sounds of someone giving you directions.**
>
> **All these examples have one thing in common:**
>
> ## *sound.*

Footsteps, the sound of the wind against your ears, a door creaking, a flushing toilet, even the sounds of someone giving you directions. All these examples have one thing in common: *sound.*

Without our auditory system, we would be unable to discriminate and decipher between sounds that are either important or just a regular part of the environment. Right now, I can hear a plane flying by, the keys of the keyboard being pressed, birds chirping outside, and the dishwasher signal going off. But if I listen closely, I also hear the whirr of the air conditioner, the cars on the street behind our house, and the ticking of the clock. Sounds surround me and because of my auditory system, I can determine which ones I should pay attention to and which ones to ignore for now.

As an educator, I remember students who refused to go to music class, covered their ears during the morning announcements, and cried during fire drills. I know now that those children were over-stimulated by auditory input.

But what about the students who seek auditory input? The ones that constantly tap their pencil on the desk, the ones that cannot use an inside voice if their life depended on it, or the ones that seem to shout out absurdities during the middle of a quiet lesson. We might label those children as "bad," "disruptive," or "disrespectful." What if I told you they had underlying reasons for doing those things? What if I told you they were seeking auditory input to help their nervous systems feel more balanced?

Then you have "those kids." You know, the ones that *never* seem to listen to a word you are saying. The ones that never seem to respond to your requests or that seem to be daydreaming and not on task. Many times, these children are struggling with an under-responsive auditory system.

Remember how I said this system baffles me? That is because with my son, we do not see just one of these behaviors – we see *all of them*. Depending on the time of day or day of the week, we might see him react to sounds in his environment in any of the ways I mentioned.

Before I learned about Sensory Processing Disorder, I never understood why my son shouted all the time. I worried he might have hearing loss or that he had an ear infection he wasn't telling us about. I remember his father being so worried because despite all our best attempts, he just seemed to shout everything at us. We cannot go to a library or a store without some stranger telling my son to be quiet and use an "inside voice." Sometimes I want to shout back at them, "He can't!"

More recently, he started avoiding certain sounds. This seems to come and go based on how balanced the rest of his systems are and how "in control" his body seems. Recently, we attempted to go out to breakfast. We picked the best place in the city, had a family walk to the restaurant, and were ready to enjoy our family time. But the minute we walked inside, my son covered his ears and started to bounce from me to my husband. To him, the restaurant was overwhelming. He heard every noise – the dishes clanging, the babies crying, the cash register clinking, the coffee pouring, the bacon sizzling, the chairs scooting. He heard all of it. We simply could not eat there, no matter how much we wanted to.

One of the most confusing behaviors I have seen with my son is his reaction to loud and over-stimulating situations. Take him to a store, a crowded area, or an assembly at school, and you unleash a totally different animal. He becomes overly excited, hyperactive, and full of energy. He becomes unmanageable. I used to dread going to any of these places with him until I learned how interconnected the vestibular and auditory senses were. Then I learned how to provide him with appropriate input before, during, and after an over-stimulating experience like the store. With the help of sound-reducing ear muffs and some swinging activities, our trips to the store are now a little more manageable. ●

CHAPTER 3

The Olfactory System

A Therapist's Perspective

The olfactory system is how we pick up information about the odors around us and pass that information along a channel of nerves, where it eventually reaches the brain. Our olfactory systems can discriminate between thousands of different odors and help us recognize whether smells are dangerous, strong, faint, pleasurable, or foul.

However, the olfactory system does more than process the odors we smell. It is also closely related to our limbic system, which is a part of our nervous system that is responsible for emotions and memory. This is why the smell of the leaves in the fall can instantly give us that "first day of school" feeling, even if we haven't been to school in years.

The olfactory system is also associated with the sense of taste, which helps to create the flavors we taste in food. This is why nothing seems to taste quite right when we have a stuffed-up nose.

A HEALTHY OLFACTORY SYSTEM

Children with healthy olfactory systems are able to tolerate smelling foods and other odors in their environments. They can even tolerate unpleasant odors (within reason) without extreme reactions. A functioning olfactory system helps children know the difference between "good" smells – those that are safe, pleasant, or associated with positive emotions – and "bad" smells – those that are dangerous, displeasing, or reminders of negative experiences. Children with well-developed olfactory systems will eagerly take part in playful activities that explore the sense of smell.

PROBLEMS WITH THE OLFACTORY SYSTEM

Children with sensory processing issues may be overly sensitive (hypersensitive) to smells. For example, these children may:

· Gag or even throw up when they encounter smells that are not offensive or even noticeable to most people
· Pick up on and become distracted by smells that most people do not notice, such as the smell of the cleaner used on their desk or the smell of the soap they used to wash their hands
· Struggle at mealtimes, both with smelling the foods on their plates and with tasting the food presented to them
· Fail to experience pleasure with smells that most of us associate with pleasant memories or good experiences, like smelling chocolate chip cookies baking in the oven

Other children demonstrate decreased sensitivity to smells (hyposensitivity). Hyposensitive children may:

· Seem to crave certain smells and frequently hold non-food items to their noses to smell them, such as crayons, toys, and so on
· Use smell to attempt to learn about their surroundings
· Fail to understand "safe" versus "dangerous" smells, which can lead to safety issues, such as being drawn to strong smells like cleaning chemicals or strong-scented permanent markers

The olfactory sense is a way for children to experience and learn about the world around them. However, for some children, difficulty with processing olfactory input can interfere with the way they enjoy and interact with their environments.

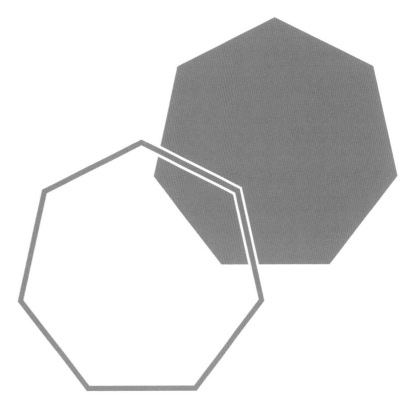

A Parent and Educator's Point of View

Compared to the other sensory systems, you won't hear or read much about the olfactory system. In fact, you might not even be familiar with this term until now. However, you have most likely experienced the effects of the olfactory system more than you realize.

The olfactory system is not simply about our ability to smell pleasant and unpleasant odors but our ability to discern and recognize safe and unsafe odors. To be successful day to day, we must use our olfactory system to notice and decipher these scents.

> **Your favorite piece of chocolate, pancakes on a Saturday morning, rotting fruit in the trash, and your grandma's perfume.**
>
> **All these examples have one thing in common:**
>
> ## *smell.*

Your favorite piece of chocolate, pancakes on a Saturday morning, rotting fruit in the trash, and your grandma's perfume. All these examples have one thing in common: *smell.*

When I think of the olfactory system, I imagine one of two things. I picture someone smelling flowers in a field with a smile on her face. She is in the moment, taking in everything around her, registering that moment in time, and making a positive memory that will last. In this scenario, she uses her sense of smell to take in information, process it, and make sense of her surroundings.

On the opposite side, I think of stench. Downright nasty smells that seem to linger and you cannot seem to get out of your nose. Can you imagine them? I bet you can even smell an unpleasant smell just by thinking about it.

The truth is our sense of smell is so much more than just a way to sense odors. It is so closely connected to our taste (gustatory) sense that it can actually improve or inhibit the way we taste things. This can be a problem – a big problem – if your child's sense of smell is heightened or decreased. It can affect your child's eating habits, working memory, and ability to recall information.

I remember an adorable 3-year-old in my blended preschool program. The very first day I met her, the way she reacted to new things shocked me. As she explored the classroom, she would smell everything! New crayon… sniff. New block…sniff. New paint…sniff. I was so confused. I would later come to learn that this little girl had Sensory Processing Disorder, which I knew absolutely nothing about at the time.

In our house, we struggle with this system more than I would like to admit. Some days, my son won't eat anything. We hear things like, "It doesn't taste right. It smells gross. I don't like it." At first, I am always frustrated. It may be something he loved the day before. It may even be one of his favorite foods. Yet for some reason, today he won't have anything to do with it. Before I learned about sensory processing, I never connected this with anything more than him being picky. However, I learned that when he has trouble with the odors around him, it affects his eating. This outward behavior tells me his sensory systems are having trouble staying organized. ●

CHAPTER 4

Oral Sensory Processing

A Therapist's Perspective

Oral sensory processing is the way our brains receive input from our mouth and jaw. When we eat or drink, our mouths send information to our brains regarding what we're eating or drinking. This information includes the temperature, texture (for example, smooth like yogurt, hard like a potato chip, or a mixture of textures like cereal with milk), and taste (sweet, salty, bitter, or sour). Our brains also receive proprioceptive information from the joints of the jaw as we bite and chew foods with different types of resistance, such as a crunchy carrot or a chewy piece of candy.

Oral sensory processing also contributes to the way we move our mouths, control our saliva production, and produce sounds for clear speech. The way our mouths perceive sensory information helps us eat and drink in a functional, adaptive way and allows us to enjoy and participate in mealtimes with family and friends.

HEALTHY ORAL SENSORY PROCESSING

Children with healthy oral sensory systems typically eat a variety of foods with a range of tastes and textures. They are willing to try new foods – within reason. Most young children tend to avoid certain foods like green leafy vegetables and certain kinds of meat. Children with healthy oral sensory systems can tolerate eating foods with mixed textures like cereal and milk or vegetable soup and also can tolerate experiences like brushing their teeth and visiting the dentist with little or no difficulty. They do not need to seek out additional oral sensory experiences such as chewing on non-food objects in order to regulate their behavior. Their everyday oral experiences already provide enough proprioceptive input to help them feel satisfied.

PROBLEMS WITH ORAL SENSORY PROCESSING

Children with oral sensory processing issues struggle with processing and responding to the oral input they encounter every day. They may have a heightened sensitivity (*hypersensitivity* or *defensiveness*) to oral input, which causes them to be resistant to experiences like trying new foods or brushing their teeth. Hypersensitive children may:

- Choke or gag
- Be described as "picky eaters"
- Have an extremely limited diet because they restrict themselves to only a few familiar foods
- Refuse to use utensils to eat because they dislike the feeling of a spoon or fork in their mouths
- Resist oral sensory experiences through extreme emotional reactions, such as tantrums, fear, or running away, which makes mealtimes and dental hygiene difficult

Some care providers may refer children with these issues to specialized feeding clinics in order to address aversions and to expand their diets and tolerances.

Other children experience decreased awareness of oral sensory input (*hyposensitivity*). Children who experience hyposensitivity may require *more* input to help them organize their behavior and pay attention. These children may:

· Bite, chew on, or mouth non-food objects, including clothing, hands, fingers, pencils, and toys
· Try to bite others
· Over-stuff their mouths with food at mealtimes
· Make frequent sounds with their mouths for extra sensory input, such as clicking, humming, and buzzing, which may annoy or distract people around them.

Decreased sensitivity to oral input can also lead to difficulty with awareness and coordination of the movements of the mouth, including difficulties with chewing or drinking from a cup or a straw. Hyposensitivity may affect oral motor planning and speech production.

Oral sensory processing is not just about the sense of taste (the gustatory sense). It also allows us to perceive a wide range of other sensory information about what we eat and drink, and it provides important proprioceptive information as well.

A Parent and Educator's Point of View

When I think back to learning about the five senses, taste was always my favorite. Learning about it meant we got to try delicious foods, learn about sweet versus salty, and test different textures. However, I never connected the sense of taste (the gustatory sense) to anything more than knowing the names of flavors and foods. The oral system is not simply about the ability to taste and discern textures in your mouth. It is so much more.

Biting, chewing, chomping, crunching, sucking, licking, and swallowing. All these activities have two things in common: *taste* and *texture*.

> Biting, chewing, chomping, crunching, sucking, licking, and swallowing.
>
> All these activities have two things in common:
>
> *taste* and *texture*.

It was not until recently that I learned about the interconnectedness of the oral sensory and proprioceptive systems. The need to chew, bite, and suck comes from the proprioceptive input you receive from the pressure in your jaw. This connection is key to helping your brain organize information, stay focused, and process the other information in your environment.

As an educator, I met a sweet 3-year-old girl who experienced the world through her oral system. Every time she picked up a block, a book, or even a crayon, she would first sniff it and then lick it three times. This same little girl was known as the class biter. She bit everyone, everything, and even herself. We spent countless hours educating other parents, her friends, and other teachers about her oral sense and her need to seek oral input. Unfortunately, others interpreted these behaviors as "bad" or "naughty" or "mean," but that was not the little girl's intention at all. She just needed something to chew. She needed us to be aware of her oral sensory system. If only I knew then what I know now, I could have helped her more.

I had another 3-year-old student who constantly drooled, put her fingers in her mouth, and never ate anything at snack time. She was the pickiest of picky eaters and from the reports of her parents, they struggled to get her to eat anything healthy. At the time, I thought her behavior was due to her parents not teaching her how to be a healthy eater because my kids were healthy eaters. I didn't have trouble getting my kids to eat, so what was wrong with these parents? Again, if only I had known what I know now. Sadly, we didn't know this child was hypersensitve to the textures, tastes, and other sensations associated with eating. It wasn't until I learned about

Sensory Processing Disorder that I found out that that "picky eating" is not necessarily a parenting or behavioral issue.

In my home, this sensory system looks a little different. My child touches and puts everything in his mouth. This child has been sick with more viruses than you could count because if the germs are there, he will get them on his hands and eat them. Ever heard of herpangina? Me neither, but now we've had it more times in our house than I care to admit, and we know everything about it. Why? Because of my son's need to sense the world through his oral sensory receptors.

"Fingers out of your mouth!"

"Stop biting that!"

"Don't put so much food in your mouth!"

You can often hear these statements in our house. Or at least you could until we learned a few ways to help my son with his need for oral stimulation.

I am a tad nervous to share one story, but I feel it is important. This occurred when my son was four, and his younger brother was only two. My older son had such an intense need to chew that he chewed off his brother's fingernail. Yes, you read that right. He chewed his brother's fingernail completely off. It was then that we realized we needed to address a bigger problem. It was beyond chewing the bed post, and it was beyond biting his own nails. Now it was affecting someone else.

The sad thing is that at the time, I was furious. How could he do such a thing to his little brother? If I had known about healthy alternatives for the need to chew and ways to provide proprioceptive input through daily routines, I might have reacted differently and gotten him the help he needed.

CHAPTER 5

The Proprioceptive System

A Therapist's Perspective

Proprioception refers to the way our joints and muscles send messages to our brains to provide information about our bodies' positioning and movement. This sense also allows us to grade the force and direction of our movements. For example, our bodies instinctively know to apply more effort when lifting a heavy box and less effort when lifting a piece of paper.

While the vestibular system tells the brain about balance and moving against gravity, the proprioceptive system helps us coordinate the movement of our arms and legs in an efficient manner to play and move without even having to look.

A HEALTHY PROPRIOCEPTIVE SYSTEM

A functioning proprioceptive system allows children to write with a pencil without pushing so hard that they break the tip or to take a drink from a plastic cup without crushing it in their hand. When the proprioceptive system is healthy, it allows children to move, play, and explore in a smoothly coordinated and efficient way – not too gentle, and not too rough.

PROBLEMS WITH PROPRIOCEPTION

When a child's proprioceptive system is not functioning correctly, they may need to seek out additional input to their muscles and joints so they can regulate their behavior and stay in control. They may:

· Be known as "rough kids" because they push others in line or play aggressively on the playground
· Have a hard time grading the force of their movements, such as using extreme pressure on their pencils and crayons

On the other hand, these children may:

· Walk rarely because they prefer to stomp, gallop, or jump everywhere they go
· Have poor body awareness, such as appearing weak and clumsy or bumping into walls or other children while walking down the hallway at school
· Struggle with maintaining upright posture so they often lean, slump, and even fall out of their chairs
· Use too *little* force during fine motor and gross motor activities, compared to other children who use too much pressure

Even though these two types of children exhibit different behaviors, they both need more proprioceptive input built into their daily routines. Proprioceptive activities provide opportunities for heavy work, such as pushing, pulling, and moving against resistance. This heavy work can help wake up or calm a child's body and mind.

A Parent and Educator's Point of View

Proprioceptive. Proprioception. Both words tie my tongue just trying to say them. To this day, I still slow down to make sure I am saying them correctly. Out of all the sensory systems, this tongue twister is a mystery to many. I never realized how many daily activities are actually tied to the proprioceptive system. Think Twister, Simon Says, or even hopscotch. All these classic games require you to use your body's sense of awareness to interpret the world around you.

Pushing, pulling, stomping, squeezing, jumping, bending. All these examples have one thing in common: *body position.*

Without your proprioceptive system, you cannot know where different parts of your body are without looking. I bet right now you could close your eyes and still touch your finger to the tip of your nose. That is because of your proprioceptive system. Every time you run up the stairs, carry a load of laundry, sit, stand, bend, or stretch, you are using your proprioceptive system.

> Pushing, pulling, stomping, squeezing, jumping, bending.
>
> All these examples have one thing in common:
>
> ## body position.

As an educator, I remember my first encounter with a little boy who would reach his arms out as far as he could. He would run through the classroom and hit everything and everyone in his path. He looked like an airplane with his wings stretched wide, coming in for a crash landing. Then one little girl would bite and hit anyone she sat next to in circle time, no matter what tactics and methods we tried. I wish I would have known at the time that these children were screaming for help. They were telling me they needed proprioceptive input.

On the flip side, I had other students who never wanted to do anything with the group. They disliked almost any activity. In fact, when we went to the playground, they would lie down. What child wants to lie down at the playground? People often use a word to describe these children. It's ugly, but people say it all the time: lazy. Sadly, no one (including me) knew that those children's brains and bodies needed more proprioceptive input in order to be an active participant in the group.

In my home, our experience with the proprioceptive system looked more like the crashing airplane boy from my classroom, except it wasn't so obvious. I thought my son was "bad" or "naughty" and used to wonder what I was doing wrong. You know how little boys typically love to wrestle and roughhouse? In my house, this simply cannot happen. The minute we begin to tickle, wrestle, or goof around, someone gets hurt. Seriously hurt. My son has no gauge for proprioceptive input. He does not know when to stop or when to resist the urge to push, pull, hit, or grab. He always takes it too far.

Then we have the chewing. Oh, the chewing. While I know most of us think of chewing as purely an oral sensory behavior, I have learned how closely related this is to the proprioceptive system. My son has successfully chewed his entire bedpost to shreds, broken all the pencils in the house (with his teeth), and even chewed off his brother's nails. Giving him supports such as chewies and gum have helped. However, his chewing needs did not decrease until we started giving him full body proprioceptive input through a regulated sensory diet.

I could go on and on about our experiences with proprioception. While I know that all the sensory systems are interconnected, this is the area where I see the most obvious signs of difficulty for my son. Until my son was seven years old, he *never* hugged me. Never. He would push on me, bury his head on me, but he *never* hugged me. But after we started occupational therapy, chiropractic care, and other interventions, he finally wanted me to hug and cuddle him. •

CHAPTER 6

The Tactile System

A Therapist's Perspective

The tactile sense is how we interpret the information we get from the receptors in our skin. When we feel an object in our environment, our nervous system receives this information and helps us understand and differentiate pressure, temperature, texture, traction, and other tactile qualities of the object. It also lets us determine exactly what it is that we are feeling.

Our tactile system also helps us understand and feel pain. The relationship between touch and the emotional centers in the brain helps us remember details about tactile experiences that are pleasurable and ones that are not pleasurable. The tactile system lets you know when the shower is warm enough (but not too hot) and helps you decide whether you prefer a calm bath or a strong shower. It's how you know you are touching something sharp, smooth, rough, or bumpy.

Touch receptors are not only in your hands – in fact, *they are all over your body*. Because of these receptors, you feel your foot hit the floor with every step or grab your favorite jeans or shirt because they feel good to wear.

A HEALTHY TACTILE SYSTEM

When the tactile system is functioning well, children are secure and organized in their bodies so they can attend and respond to all the sensory information they encounter each day. They do not become distracted by the constant tactile input they experience in any given moment, such as the way their shirt feels on their arms, the feeling of the breeze hitting their face, and so on. This is because they can filter out which tactile information is important and which is not.

Children with well-developed tactile systems engage in play easily with their peers and explore toys during parallel and group play. The tactile system is what lets children reach way down into their toy box and pull out their favorite action figure without even looking. They effortlessly participate in everyday activities like bathing, brushing teeth, washing hands, dressing and tolerating clothing, and mealtime routines. They show curiosity by feeling and interacting with their environment throughout the day in a controlled manner. They are not fearful of touching or being touched, and they are not preoccupied with touching everything around them.

PROBLEMS WITH TACTILE PROCESSING

Some children experience difficulty with processing the tactile information they encounter in everyday life. They may be overly sensitive (*hypersensitive*) to tactile input, causing them to withdraw from or avoid certain tactile experiences. To children with tactile hypersensitivity, even the most basic touch experiences may be unpleasant or even painful. Children who are hypersensitive to tactile input may:

- Avoid getting their hands or faces messy
- Steer away from activities like finger painting, playdough, and even eating certain foods
- Struggle with certain hygiene tasks and have extreme reactions or tantrums during toothbrushing, bathing, and haircuts
- Find it difficult to tolerate certain types of clothing

Other children may have the opposite experience by demonstrating decreased awareness of tactile input (*hyposensitivity*). They may seek out more tactile input to give their bodies what they need. These children may:

- Love to touch and be touched
- Crave hugs, sit very closely to others, and seek out different textures and touch experiences
- "Fiddle" with objects in their hands, such as rubbing them, turning them over and over, and squeezing them
- Seem fearless because they touch everything they see, even objects that might be dangerous
- Be less aware of the tactile input they come into contact with, such as not noticing when their hands or faces are messy at mealtimes
- Fail to react to or show preferences for certain types of tactile experiences

The ability to process tactile input is important so children can regulate their behavior, maintain attention to play and learning activities, and engage and participate in functional tasks throughout the day.

A Parent and Educator's Point of View

The word "tactile" is one you might have heard before, even if you are unfamiliar with sensory processing. Before learning about sensory processing, I always thought "tactile" meant one thing: *hands-on learning*. Little did I know it means so much more. Your ability to process tactile input is directly related to your ability to visually discriminate, motor plan, and practice appropriate body awareness. More importantly, the tactile system is invaluable for developing emotional security and social skills as well as for academic learning.

> **Hugs, clothing, the grass or sand under your feet, the food you eat, the coffee you drink.**
>
> **All these examples have one thing in common:**
>
> ***touch.***

Hugs, clothing, the grass or sand under your feet, the food you eat, the coffee you drink. All these examples have one thing in common: *touch.*

When you think of the word "tactile," what image comes to mind? For many, it is an image of children getting messy. It is playing in the sand, feeling a soft animal, running hands through cold water, or learning through touch. Your perception of the world is affected by the way your tactile system interprets it.

As an educator, I remember vividly children who would suddenly (without any clear reason) reach out and pinch, hit, or push another child. They were not mad. They were not being mean. Their tactile systems needed more input. Other children who were having issues with tactile sensory processing would refuse to sit in their seats. I remember one student who never sat down. He could not explain his need to stand because he didn't understand why he had difficulty sitting down. Sadly, neither did I.

During my training as a teacher, I learned behavior and classroom management strategies to deal with these behaviors. However, no one taught me strategies to provide children with the sensory input they required to be successful in the classroom. In fact, I did not realize these behaviors were more than just poor behavior management until my own son started getting older, and it was no longer age-appropriate for him to eat with his hands or hit his brother on the head as he walked by.

He had always been fidgety, touched everything, had poor impulse control, and had extreme mood swings. But most times, I thought some of these behaviors were happening because I was a bad mom. Now, I know more. I know that my son's behaviors are due to his sensory processing needs and deficits, and they are not related to something I am doing wrong. I can take steps to support and help him.

Some of my most vivid memories are of trying to get my son out the door for school each morning. I remember him yelling, crying, screaming, throwing tantrums, and having meltdowns. All of this over…socks. They hurt. They did not feel good. They irritated him. I will never forget the day he came down the stairs and told me, "Mom, I can't find any happy socks." My heart melted.

Learning about the tactile system through my son's occupational therapists and from helpful online resources allowed me to see his behaviors in a new way. I can find ways to provide the input his body needs. Refer to the Sensory Resources section of this book for a list of these resources. ●

CHAPTER 7

The Vestibular System

A Therapist's Perspective

The vestibular sense has to do with balance and movement and is centered in the inner ear. Each of us has vestibular organs located deep inside our ears. When we move our heads, the fluid in these organs moves and shifts, which constantly provides us with information about the position of our heads and bodies in space (*spatial awareness*).

This sense allows us to maintain our balance and to experience gravitational security: confidence that we can maintain a position without falling. The vestibular system helps us move smoothly and efficiently. It also works alongside all our other sensory systems by helping us use our eyes effectively and process sounds in our environment. Overall, vestibular processing helps us feel confident moving and interacting with our surroundings.

A HEALTHY VESTIBULAR SYSTEM

When the vestibular system is fully functioning, children are secure and organized in their bodies so they can attend and respond to all the other sensory input they encounter daily. Children with well-developed vestibular systems feel confident and safe during movement activities, even if their feet are off the ground. They can start and stop movement activities calmly and with control. They are comfortable with climbing, swinging, somersaulting, and jumping because they know their bodies will adapt. This security enables them to maintain their balance and keep from falling or getting hurt.

PROBLEMS WITH VESTIBULAR PROCESSING

A healthy vestibular system is central to the integration of the other sensory systems. When children's vestibular systems are not functioning correctly, they may be under responsive (*hyposensitive*) or overly sensitive (*hypersensitive*) to movement. They may:

- Need to move constantly to feel satisfied or be fearful of movement because it makes them feel insecure and unbalanced
- Move in an uncoordinated, clumsy manner, such as bumping into things, falling, and never fully walking or sitting in an upright manner
- Slouch at their desks or need constant redirection to "stand up straight" or "quit leaning on the wall"
- Appear weak or "floppy"
- Have difficulty coordinating and planning motor tasks such as jumping jacks, skipping, catching a ball with two hands, reaching across the center of their bodies (*midline crossing*), or even coordinating movements of the mouth, which results in difficulty with speech production

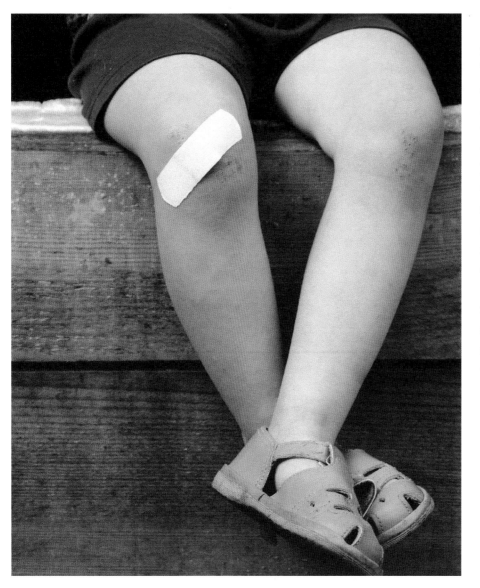

In addition, vision is closely related to the vestibular system. When children feel balanced and centered, their eyes can move smoothly and steadily and are able to focus, track, and discriminate between objects in their environments. Difficulty with tasks that require the eyes to move left to right (such as reading) or up and down repeatedly (such as copying information from the board) may be signs of a disrupted vestibular system.

Functional vestibular processing is essential for children to feel a sense of security about movement and about where they are in relation to their surroundings.

A Parent and Educator's Point of View

To me, the word "vestibular" sounds weird. It is scary and intimidating. In fact, I had not even heard of this sensory system before learning about sensory processing. Because of my journey with my son, I now understand the importance of the vestibular sense. What comes to mind is all the rides at a fair: the tilt-a-whirl, the Ferris wheel, the jungle gyms, and even the pirate ship.

Spinning, turning, flipping, climbing. These sensations all have one thing in common: *movement.*

As an educator, I remember being confused by how some children could not attend to a lesson without bouncing, fidgeting, or rocking. One student fell out of his seat on a regular basis, despite all attempts to help him "sit correctly." I also witnessed the opposite end of the spectrum: the children who refused to play freeze dance with the rest of the class, the children who were hesitant to take risks like climbing on the playground, or the children who were sedentary. If you didn't know better, you might call these children "lazy." No one ever taught me about the vestibular system when I was an educator. When my own son started getting older and it was no longer age-appropriate for him to be spinning in circles or moving at full speed everywhere we went, I realized I needed to learn more.

> Spinning, turning, flipping, climbing.
>
> These sensations all have one thing in common:
>
> # *movement.*

It is not unheard of for my son to place his head on the ground and spin in circles. If we are trying to talk about something important, this kind of behavior escalates. We struggle with impulse control on a daily basis, and until we started receiving therapy for his sensory needs, it was downright scary. At times, other people were hurt because my son could not control his impulsive habits.

I used to pass off his impulsiveness as a behavioral issue. Again, I questioned my parenting skills. To give you an idea of the types of behavior I am talking about, let me share a few of the incidents burned into my memory. One time, he turned on the lawn mower when his dad was fixing it. He once stepped on the golf cart pedal and ran into his aunt. Another time, he pushed his brother off the top of the slide without realizing he had done it. Every time, he felt awful. Every time, he did not even know how the incident had happened. My son moves so fast that he often doesn't have time to think about the consequences of his actions or stop his impulses. •

CHAPTER 8

The
Visual
System

A Therapist's Perspective

The visual system is how we receive and process sensory information through our eyes. The eyes and the brain communicate and work together to help us interpret our physical surroundings using what we see. When we see an object, it is because of the perception of light. Light rays follow a path through the many different structures of our eyes, eventually relaying visual information to the visual cortex in our brains. Here, the brain identifies the object and gives it meaning. We are able to perceive details like color, three-dimensional depth perception, and the location of the object in space. Our visual system allows us to create a memory of the image and gives the image context within our environment.

Vision is closely integrated with all our other senses. If we see freshly baked cookies, we become hungry as our sense of smell and our taste buds kick in. If we see a large spider, our tactile system goes to work. We get goose bumps and may feel a sense of fear. Vision helps us process, understand, and take action in our environments. If you look around, you will see thousands of images and details in every direction.

A HEALTHY VISUAL SYSTEM

When the visual system is fully functioning, children automatically focus on the details in their environment that are most important so they can filter out the ones that are not important. For example, during a game of hide and seek, children filter out most of what they see around them except that bulky chair they know will make a great hiding spot. When children walk into their classroom after recess, they automatically scan the room and head right to their seats.

Imagine that the visual system is a bike wheel. At the center of the wheel is the ability to see. All the spokes coming off the center are the many different aspects of vision, including visual discrimination, visual acuity, visual memory, visual form, visual motor abilities, and so on. The various functions of the visual system help our children grow, learn, and develop.

PROBLEMS WITH VISUAL PROCESSING

Some children are highly distracted by the visual stimuli around them (*hypersensitive*). They may:

· Be overwhelmed by the many colors in the room, the posters or art on the walls, and the movement of others around them
· See activity outside the window or want to count the tiles on the floor that are different colors and textures
· Fail to focus on a task like coloring a picture because of all these visual distractions

On the other hand, children who are visually under stimulated (*hyposensitive*) may barely notice their surroundings unless details and objects are pointed out to them. They may:

· Stare at the same point for extended periods of time
· Quickly become confused during visual activities and lose interest.

These children need a visual boost.

A Parent and Educator's Point of View

The visual system is somewhat self-explanatory. Even if you are not familiar with sensory processing, you might have heard the term *visual input*. The visual system is one of the first systems we are taught about in school. We learn to use our sense of sight to see, observe, and make connections. However, we are not always taught the importance this system plays in our body's ability to feel in control and centered. In fact, many can overlook this system because it seems so basic. The visual system is not simply about our ability to see (20/20 vision) but also includes our ability to track, locate, and discriminate between things around us.

Determining the tint of our shirt to wear for the day, finding our socks in the sock drawer, tracking the teacher as she walks around the room. All these examples have one thing in common: *sight.*

Without a regulated visual system, you cannot focus on the important details that help you understand the world around you. Currently, books, pens, my water bottle, some loose papers, and a leftover snack surround me. Because my visual system is intact, I am still able to focus on the computer screen and write these words. Because of my visual system, I can focus on and decipher which items surrounding me are important and which ones I can ignore.

As an educator, I had a child in my class who would never look me in the eye. In fact, she would cover her eyes as I talked to her or when something important happened in the classroom. At first glance, this behavior seems like disrespect. It seemed as though she did not care at all about what I was saying, when in fact she was over-stimulated and most likely needed some of the visual stimuli to be removed.

On the other hand, some children just stared. Not at me, but out the window, at the bright lights, or at the flickering fluorescent light. They seemed to fixate on one thing. These were the same children drawn to the light table during center time, and they would act overly protective of that space if another child tried to join them.

> **Determining the tint of our shirt to wear for the day, finding our socks in the sock drawer, tracking the teacher as she walks around the room.**
>
> **All these examples have one thing in common:**
>
> ***sight.***

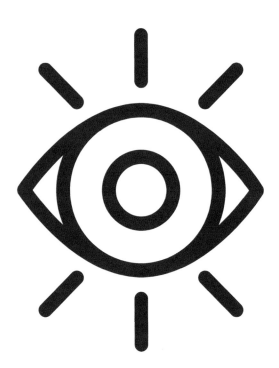

I know all parents struggle with their children locating and finding things. This is a "normal" problem to have. However, in our house, my son struggles with this on another level. Have you ever heard the phrase, "If it was a snake, it would have bitten you?" We used to joke around and call my son "Snake Bite" because he could never find *anything*, despite it being in plain sight and obvious to everyone else. We thought it was funny that he was incapable of finding anything in the mix of things, until we realized the problem was much more severe. When a child is looking for a shoe or a sock, you do not worry as much. When it starts to affect the way they function on a day-to-day basis, you realize they might need help in this area.

My son did not look me in the eye until he was seven years old. Even to this day, we struggle with eye contact and getting our son's full attention. Often times, he completely misses our facial expressions that show our moods and our instructions.

My son is a visual seeker, which means he constantly looks for objects that are visually stimulating to help regulate his nervous system. Unfortunately, this means he seeks out the television and video games. I am not opposed to giving him electronic time; in fact, we encourage some screen time. The problem comes when we unplug. It started a long time ago. We noticed that anytime he had visual input for a prolonged period of time, it would greatly affect his mood. Saturday morning cartoons are unheard of in this house because we know just how awful the day could be after a morning of cartoons.

We struggle with finding a balance because the visual stimulus is something he seeks and desires, but he has such a hard time transitioning away from being "plugged in." What we do know is that if we want to get his full attention, we need to remove all visual stimuli, and we need to get down on his level and make sure he knows we are talking to him. We have to be completely aware at all times of his surroundings and what visual stimuli he has in his environment.

Remember: *sensory processing is complex*. It is different for every child because every child is unique. ●

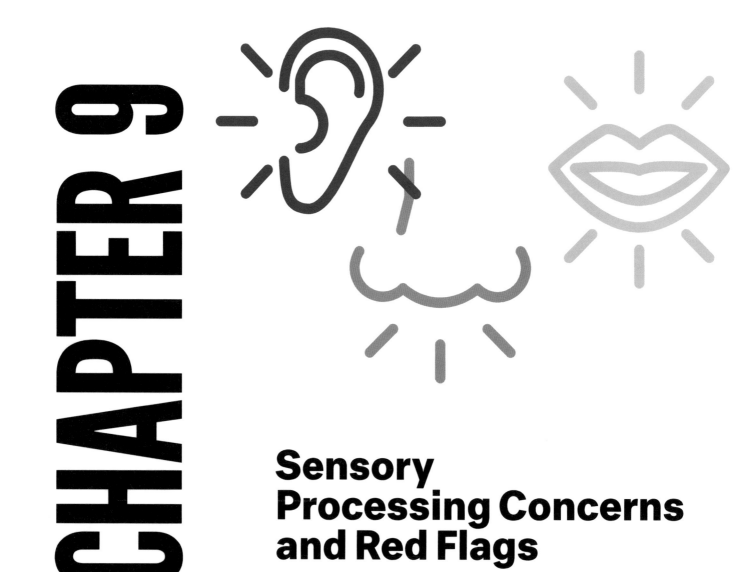

CHAPTER 9

Sensory Processing Concerns and Red Flags

Is It Just a Phase?
A Parent's Perspective

Have you ever wondered if your child's behaviors are "normal"? Or maybe people always tell you:

· "It's just a phase,"

· "He'll grow out of it," or

· "Maybe you should change your parenting."

Yet something in your gut does not feel right about your child's behaviors.

As you observe your child around others, you might start to ask yourself some questions:

· *How can I tell when it's not "just a phase?"*

· *At what point do I need to seek help for these behaviors?*

· *When will I know something serious is going on?*

· *How do I even begin to help my child?*

· *What have I done wrong?*

If any of this sounds familiar, you are not alone. In fact, other parents, educators, and caregivers are out there looking for the exact same answers you are. I know because I am one of those moms. I know because I was one of those educators. Using what I've learned, I want to help you sort through those questions and get started in the right direction.

3 Signs Your Child's Behaviors Are Not Just a Phase

I spent the first seven years of my son's life blaming myself. I cannot even begin to count the number of times I called my best friend crying and asking her what I was doing wrong. If only I could go back in time and tell myself it wasn't me. It wasn't my parenting. It wasn't my teaching. It was so much more.

Looking back over the first seven years of his life, I now see the signs. I see what I wish I had seen earlier.

SIGN 1: YOUR CHILD'S BEHAVIORS IMPACT, IMPEDE, OR GREATLY CHANGE DAILY ROUTINES

All children have some troubling behaviors, some sensory needs, and some concerns you need to address. The problem occurs when these behaviors significantly affect your child's life. In our case, our son was unable to make friends, and he was impulsive to the point of sending his dad to the hospital and running over his aunt with a golf cart. He was struggling to regulate his behaviors and would bite his nails, and he eventually bit his brother's nails to the nail bed.

SIGN 2: OTHERS CONSTANTLY COMMENT ON YOUR PARENTING, YOUR CHILD'S BEHAVIORS, OR A COMBINATION OF THE TWO

We heard it *all*.

From the time my son was an infant and we never imagined anything was "different" about him to the time he was in school and we were told, "If you just put him over your knee," we heard it all. As a baby and toddler, he needed a strict routine, and others balked at our parenting choices. After he entered school, the comments and concerns did not end there. We were told his behavior stemmed from us letting him "run all over us" and from us "not setting limits." The problem with those statements was that we were already following all the typical parenting rules. We were already doing everything the books said to do, and it was not helping. We turned to listening to anything people said because we were willing to try anything.

We were looking for answers. Unfortunately, a quick change to our parenting approach was not the answer. We needed to learn more about our son's needs.

SIGN 3: NO INTERVENTIONS, TRICKS, OR BOOKS SEEM TO BE THE ANSWER

We tried it *all*.

As much as I did not believe in spanking, we tried it. We tried time-outs. We tried reward charts even though I despise reward charts. We tried teacher tricks. We tried parenting tricks. We read articles. We read parenting books. We did it all. Nothing worked. Our son still struggled. Unfortunately, for those seven years, I blamed myself. Even though deep down I thought the problem was more complex, I never trusted myself enough to look for help. We kept thinking he would grow out of it. We thought one day he would "mature."

But he never did.

It was not until I had children with Sensory Processing Disorder in my classroom that I started to recognize the red flags associated with sensory processing problems. I began to keep notes on my son's behaviors to get to the bottom of what was going on and to learn more about how I could support his needs.

Red Flags: Recognizing Sensory Problems in Children
A Therapist's Perspective

We all have our own unique preferences and aversions when it comes to the way we perceive sensory information in our surroundings. Even as adults, we have unique sensory preferences and needs. For example, you might hate the feel of a wool sweater on your skin. You might avoid seeing a movie at the theater because it's too loud. You might avoid large crowds because you hate being touched or bumped.

When these preferences and aversions become so significant that they interfere with a child participating in everyday activities and routines, it may be time to get help.

Does your child have difficulty with any of the following activities and routines?

- Interacting with others
- Participating successfully at school
- Going out in public
- Tolerating basic self-care and grooming experiences, such as taking a bath or shower, brushing teeth, or getting dressed
- Attending family and other social events
- Eating a healthy diet and maintaining a healthy weight
- Getting an adequate amount of sleep

WHAT TO DO NEXT

Talk to your pediatrician to get a referral to an occupational therapist who is trained to evaluate children's specific sensory needs, provide therapeutic intervention to address them, and give you strategies and suggestions to use at home.

The following pages contain lists of red flag behaviors related to sensory processing and are meant as a guide to help you document any concerns you may have about your child. If you do have concerns regarding your child's sensory processing needs, we suggest you make a copy of the printable version of these lists (located in the appendix), observe your child over the course of several days, and take notes on the behaviors you observe and the circumstances in which you observe them. The lists may be helpful to share with your child's teachers, pediatrician, and/or therapists.

These lists do not contain all possible behaviors associated with sensory processing problems. Also, remember that these behaviors do not always indicate Sensory Processing Disorder. Everyone has their own unique sensory preferences, which is part of normal development. It is only when these preferences negatively influence a child's ability to function that they need intervention.

If your child requires a full evaluation, consult an occupational therapist or another medical professional to conduct a more comprehensive assessment.

Sensory Processing Red Flag Behaviors
A Therapist's Perspective

This section lists common red flag behaviors that may indicate sensory processing concerns.

You can also refer to the printable checklist in the *Sensory Resources* section of this book. Therapists can use this checklist to get a quick snapshot of a child's sensory needs during classroom or clinic observations. Parents or teachers can use the checklist to document observations of a child's behavior to share with a therapist or pediatrician.

The Auditory System

☐ Exhibiting extreme reactions (such as crying, screaming, or running away) or significant difficulty with tolerating sudden noises, specific noises, crowds, and/or loud noises

☐ Startling easily or becoming agitated in noisy environments

☐ Being distracted by all sounds

☐ Covering ears at the anticipation of a sound or in uncertain/unfamiliar environments

☐ Having difficulty responding to and following directions presented verbally

☐ Making constant noises, such as singing, humming, and/or clicking

☐ Not responding when name is called

The Oral and Olfactory Sensory Systems

☐ Being very reluctant to try new foods or being known as an extremely picky eater

☐ Demonstrating extreme resistance to oral sensory experiences like brushing teeth

☐ Refusing to use utensils to eat

☐ Choking or gagging during eating or brushing teeth

☐ Constant biting, chewing on, or mouthing hands, clothing, fingers, toys, and/or other objects

☐ Biting others

☐ Constantly making mouth noises, such as clicking, buzzing, and/or humming

☐ Stuffing mouth with food at mealtimes

☐ Having difficulty with chewing or drinking from a cup or straw

☐ Displaying constant movements of the mouth, such as moving tongue, tapping teeth, and/or rubbing lips

☐ Having strong aversions to certain smells (food or non-food)

☐ Seeking out specific smells regardless of safety (food or non-food)

☐ Frequently smelling non-food objects

The Proprioceptive System

☐ Coloring or writing with heavy pressure or not enough pressure

☐ Pushing others or playing aggressively

☐ Doing everything with 100 percent force and not grading the force of movements adequately

☐ Crashing or falling on the floor constantly throughout the day

☐ Having difficulty with body awareness, such as running into objects or others

☐ Appearing tired or sluggish, such as slumping and/or leaning

The Tactile System

☐ Avoiding getting hands or face messy

☐ Avoiding activities like finger painting, playing with playdough, and eating messy foods

☐ Exhibiting extreme reactions or tantrums during toothbrushing, bathing, haircuts, and/or dressing

☐ Having difficulty tolerating certain clothing or textures on skin, such as tags on clothing

☐ Needing to touch everything and everyone, such as craving hugs and closeness with others, fidgeting with objects, and/or seeking out textures and touch experiences

The Vestibular System

- [ ] Constantly moving, fidgeting, and/or spinning around
- [ ] Being fearful of movement, such as stairs, playground equipment, or swings
- [ ] Acting uncoordinated or clumsy, which includes bumping into things, falling, or having difficulty learning new motor tasks
- [ ] Slumping, slouching, or leaning on desk or on walls when walking in the hallway
- [ ] Having difficulty with maintaining balance when walking and during physically active play
- [ ] Having difficulty with visual activities such as focus or tracking

The Visual System

- [ ] Being easily distracted by surrounding visual stimuli, such as posters or art on the walls, activity in the room, and so on
- [ ] Having difficulty visually focusing on a task like coloring a picture or completing a worksheet
- [ ] Not noticing surroundings unless others point them out
- [ ] Staring intently at objects or becoming fixated on visual stimuli, such as fans, lights, and so on
- [ ] Arranging objects in a specific way repeatedly, such as lining up objects and/or stacking objects

Moving Beyond "Just a Phase" and Getting Help
A Parent's Perspective

If you read the signs and red flags and found yourself nodding along, you are one step closer to getting help. Follow these steps to get a little closer.

STEP 1: TRUST YOUR GUT

You are the parent. You are the grandparent. You are the educator. If you feel something is not quite right, speak up. If you feel like you or someone else could be doing more to help your child succeed, speak up. Over the last few years in our journey, we have noticed one recurring theme among parents we met along the way. They all wish they had just trusted their instincts. Often times, if they think back (like I did), they can see so many signs staring them in the face.

Maybe you were not even the first one to notice the signs of something different. Maybe a teacher, another parent, or even a doctor planted the seed in your head. Whatever the case is, you know your child. You know if this is more than "just a phase," and you have to trust that.

To be clear, *I am not advocating for over diagnosing.* However, I am suggesting if you have a gut feeling about your child, follow that feeling and look for answers.

STEP 2: FIND ANSWERS

This is probably the most difficult part of the process. You might be wondering where to even start. I will share what we did to find answers. However, this is an ongoing journey. We are always seeking new strategies and resources. We are constantly perplexed and trying new things, because the truth is: this is not a pretty ride. It may have open doors, shut doors, and entire buildings locked up tight. I urge you to keep searching, and you will find the answers you need.

Tips for Navigating Your Journey to Getting Help

- Talk with other parents, educators, and child specialists. Get recommendations for helpful books, websites, and resources to get you started.
- Talk to your child's teachers, caregivers, and anyone who is around the child frequently. Which behaviors concern them and why? Write these down somewhere so you have them later down the road when you have to fill out countless forms.
- Read, read, and read some more. In our case, we needed to read more about Sensory Processing Disorder, as many of the behaviors we saw pointed right to SPD.
- Reference checklists and common red flag behaviors that could help you determine the significance of your child's needs.
- Speak to your child's pediatrician and get a referral for an occupational therapy (OT) or a neuropsychological evaluation. Note that this part can get sticky when insurance becomes involved.
- Discuss your child's evaluations, needs, and accommodations with the school.

While this book mainly refers to Sensory Processing Disorder and sensory needs, there are several diagnoses and special circumstances to consider for your child. This could include disorders such as ASD (Autism Spectrum Disorder), SPD (Sensory Processing Disorder), ADHD (Attention Deficit Hyperactivity Disorder), and many more. This book is not meant to diagnose your child. Instead, it is meant to encourage you to look for the answers you need to help your child be successful.

STEP 3: FIND SUPPORT

This may not be an easy process. You may meet plenty of people (even professionals) who do not understand your child's needs. It may get frustrating, and some days you might even want to throw in the towel. You might not feel like fighting any more. That is where you need help. You need be able to have a group of people, a friend, or a therapist who understands what you are going through and can lift you up when you are down.

When we started this process a year ago, I knew I wanted a place where I could find support. I was tired of crying by myself, and I was tired of feeling alone. That is why I started the Support for Sensory Needs Facebook group. In this group, parents, educators, and caregivers can find support, so they do not feel so alone. This is not the only support group available. In the appendix, you will find some of our favorite places where we found answers and support.

Through support groups, you can ask questions, find answers, and feel comforted that you are not alone. Having an army of people behind you will be essential if you discover your child needs extra support in school. Support groups will help you with resources and even advocates that can help you learn the laws in your state.

STEP 4: ONCE AGAIN, TRUST YOUR GUT

At times along this road, you will feel lost, confused, and downright defeated. I urge you to remember to trust your gut. You started on this journey for a reason. You went down this path to learn more about your child because you needed answers. I want you to remember that feeling of urgency, and I want you to believe in yourself. I want you to stop blaming yourself.

You are doing the best job you know how to do right now, and that is what counts. The more you know about sensory processing, the better you can support your child and watch her thrive in her environment.

And remember: you are not alone. ●

SENSORY
ACTIVITIES

AUDITORY
ACTIVITIES

Sound Lab

Setup for this auditory play idea is easy. Create a "sound lab" and intrigue your children with the power of sound.

Instructions

1. Place all the buckets and containers in a large bin, then place all the other objects in another bin nearby. For this simple play, you do not need to provide much direction, as you will want to see how your child explores the various materials on his own.

2. Start off by showing your child how to turn the containers upside down inside the bin, like drums. Then show her how to make different sounds by dropping the different materials onto the overturned containers.

3. Let imagination take over – your child may want to turn the containers right side up or even sideways. She may want to find other objects around the house to drop on the containers. She may have other ideas for containers to use as drums.

Materials

- Two large bins
- Containers of various sizes and materials
  · Plastic containers
  · Metal baking dish
  · Aluminum trays
  · Paper plates
  · Buckets
- Materials to drop
  · Bells
  · Balls
  · Cotton balls
  · Rocks
  · Marbles

TIPS

- This activity is great for exploring soft and hard sounds or loud and quiet sounds.

- Ask your child to describe some of the sounds that she made. Which containers and objects made the loudest sounds? Which were the quietest? Which combination was her favorite?

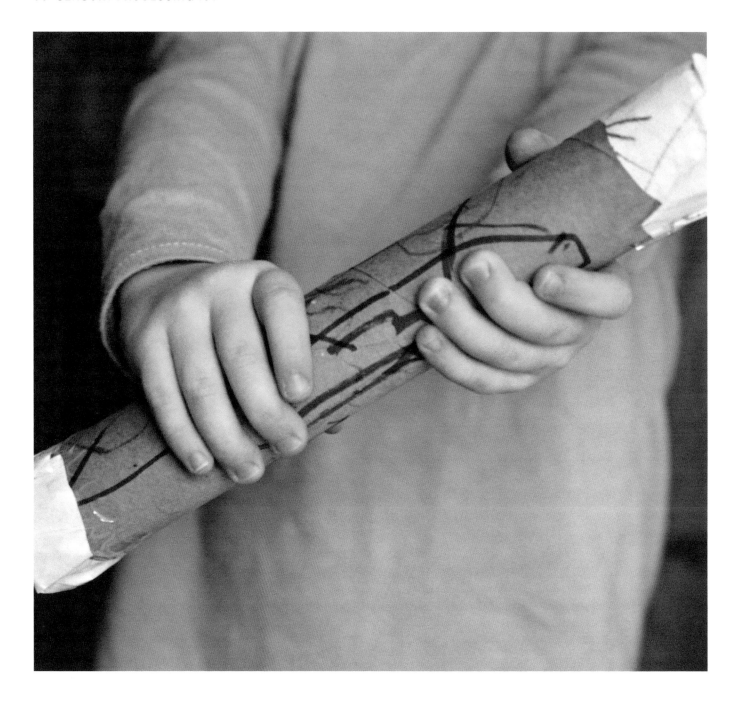

DIY Rainstick

Soothing sounds like rain falling can be a great addition to your child's nighttime or quiet time routine. A simple rainstick like this one makes a soothing rain sound even when the sun is shining.

Materials

- Empty paper towel tube
- Aluminum foil
- Dry rice
- Tape
- Paper
- Markers or paint
- A funnel (optional)

Instructions

1. Have the child decorate the paper towel tube however he likes using markers or paint.

2. Cut a circle from the piece of paper that is two inches wider than the diameter of the paper towel tube. Place the paper circle at one end of the paper towel tube and fold it upward, sealing one end of the tube. Use your tape to secure it tightly around the tube.

3. Tear off a 4- to 6-inch section of aluminum foil. Tear or cut this piece of aluminum foil into strips (lengthwise) about 1½ inches wide. Do not worry if they rip or are not perfect – they will still work.

4. Twist the strips of aluminum foil into coils and drop them into the tube until the tube is filled with foil coils but not packed too tightly.

5. Add dry rice using the funnel. Experiment with the sound by adding more or less rice or by adding or taking out aluminum foil coils.

6. Seal the other end of your tube with another paper circle and tape.

TIPS

- Allow your child to use his rainstick as a calming sensory experience before bed or during quiet time.

- Ask him to count to see how many seconds it takes the rice to fall from one end of the tube to the other.

Drumming Activities

Do you have a little one who just cannot stop making noise? Humming, yelling, singing, or chatting all day long? Or maybe you have a budding drummer who cannot seem to stop tapping – fingers, feet, or pencils.

This set of activities provides an auditory exploration experience as well as a healthy dose of proprioceptive input.

Instructions

1. **Red Light, Green Light:** Here's a fun way to experiment with tempo.
   a. Everyone begins the game by tapping at a medium speed on the table with their hands.
   b. One person acts as the leader and yells out "red light" or "green light." "Red light" means everyone has to stop tapping as quickly as they can. "Green light" means everyone has to tap as fast as they can
   c. Try throwing in "yellow light" to direct everyone to tap at a medium speed.

2. **Repeat My Rhythm:** Start by tapping out a simple rhythm on the table – just a few taps. See if the kids can imitate the rhythm. As you continue to play, try making the rhythms more and more complex. Let the kids take turns acting as the leader.

TIPS

- Try these same games using different sounds, such as clapping, snapping fingers, stomping feet, or clicking your tongue.

- Try the games using different objects as drumsticks, such as pencils, chopsticks, and so on.

Blindfold Navigation

This activity makes listening fun as kids explore their environment together. The only catch is that one friend is blindfolded. Kids have to tune into their sense of hearing to be successful with this playful challenge.

Materials

- Something to use as a blindfold
- Stuffed animals or other toys
- Basket or other container

Instructions

1. Designate a clear, safe space for this activity and be sure to have an adult supervising.

2. Children take turns being a leader and a follower. When it is the child's turn to follow, he is blindfolded – no peeking.

3. The leader gives the blindfolded friend verbal directions to move around the room. For example, he might say, "Take 4 steps forward" or "Turn to your right." You may need to assist the leading child with his directions until he catches on.

4. After they practice a bit, give the blindfolded follower a stuffed animal or other toy and see if the leader can direct the follower from a designated starting area to a basket or container on the other side of the room to put the toy inside.

TIPS

- Start by practicing without the blindfold, which allows kids to listen to the directions and see where they're going.

- Try adding some soft obstacles like pillows for the child to navigate around.

Make Your Own Rainstorm

In this fun activity, kids get to create their own thunderstorm from start to finish – using only their bodies.

This is a great way to explore sound while also working on body awareness and proprioception.

Instructions

Lead your child or group of children through the progression of a thunderstorm by saying each of the following phrases and guiding them to perform the associated movements.

"What's that? I think it's starting to rain!"
[Snap fingers slowly to sound like big, fat raindrops starting to fall.]

"Uh oh! It's really starting to come down now!"
[Slap hands on legs at medium speed to sound like rain starting to fall faster.]

"I hear the wind blowing louder and louder!"
[Rub hands together quickly.]

"I think this might turn into a thunderstorm!"
[Slap hands on legs as fast as you can.]

"Do you hear that thunder?"
[Clap hands loudly to sound like big claps of thunder.]

"I think the rain is starting to die down now."
[Slap hands on legs a little slower.]

"It sounds like the thunder is getting further and further away."
[Stomp feet on floor gently to sound like thunder rumbling in the distance.]

"And there are the last few raindrops, falling from the sky."
[Snap fingers again slowly to sound like the last raindrops of the storm.]

TIPS

– See if your child or group of children can add some of their own sounds to the storm, such as stomping in the puddles or windshield wipers sloshing back and forth.

OLFACTORY ACTIVITIES

Scented Science Experiment

Science is an easy way to integrate sensory play into your child's learning. Your kids will love exploring scents while developing their scientific skills in this simple activity.

Materials

- Vegetable oil
- Oils or extracts, such as apple, cherry, peppermint, cinnamon, vanilla and almond
- Small containers

Instructions

1. In each container, mix a ¼ cup oil and 1 tablespoon of each scent. For younger children, start with just three scents. Older children will love the challenge of guessing multiple scents.

2. After your scents are mixed, have your child waft the air above each container toward his nose and guess the scent.

3. Ask questions such as:
   - How would you describe the smell?
   - Is it sweet or sour?
   - Is it strong or weak?
   - Is it spicy?
   - Does it remind you of anything?

4. Finally, ask the child if he can guess what the smell is. How many can they guess correctly?

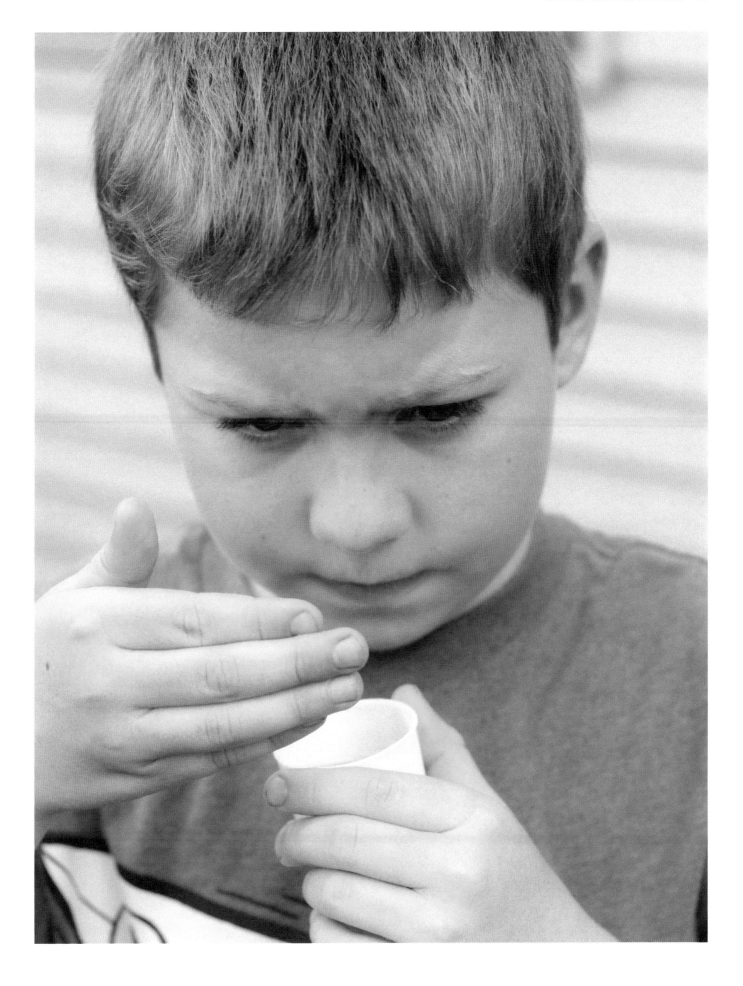

DIY Diffuser Necklaces

Scents and smells can have a significant impact on our emotions and behavior. When we find a scent we love, we want to take it everywhere with us. With these DIY diffuser necklaces, you and your child can wear your "happy scent."

Instructions

1. On a non-stick surface, roll out a small amount of air-drying clay. Roll the clay until it is 1/3 inch thick. (If the clay ends up too thin, it will become brittle when dry.)

2. Using your cookie cutters, cut the clay into circles or any small shape.

3. Use your stamps and skewers to make designs and impressions on your pendants.

4. After you have the design you like, use the skewer to make a small hole at the top of the pendant for your string to go through.

5. Let your clay dry for at least 24 hours.

6. When the clay is dry, string the pendant on your favorite necklace chain such as a string or leather strip.

7. When you are ready to wear your scent, place 1-2 drops of essential oils on the pendant and let it dry before wearing it.

Materials

- Air drying terra cotta or white clay
- Stamps
- Wooden skewer
- Small cookie cutters
- String, leather strips or necklace chain
- Essential oils

TIPS

- In the *Sensory Resource* section of this book you will find a printable guide to calming and alerting scents. You can use this guide to determine which scents you may want to add to your necklaces.

Smell and Feel

The sense of smell is a powerful thing — so powerful that we can create images in our minds without even seeing or touching the items we smell. This simple activity encourages children to make connections between real-life objects and those those mental images created by smell.

Materials
– Blindfold
– Empty containers
– Cotton balls
– Scented oils or extracts, such as lemon, apple, licorice, cinnamon, orange, and so on
– Real life objects to match each scent, such as lemons, apples, and so on

Instructions

1. Sprinkle 1-2 drops of each oil or extract on a cotton ball and place one cotton ball in each container.

2. Place the real-life objects on a table in front of your child. Discuss what she sees and the names of each of the items.

3. Blindfold your child.

4. Give her one of the scented containers to smell and have her feel her way around the table to find the matching object.

TIPS

– For younger children, try using very familiar scents to start such as banana, orange, and berry.

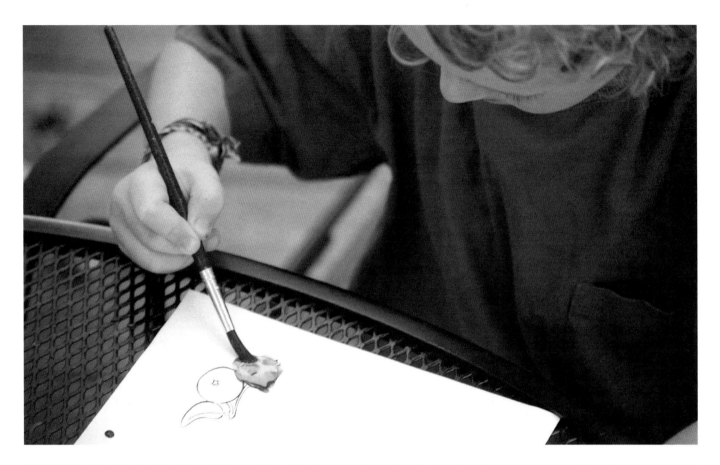

DIY Scratch 'n' Sniff Stickers

Scratch 'n sniff stickers are a staple of childhood. You can use them on schoolwork or at home, and with this DIY version, you can make a variety of different scents according to your child's preferences.

Materials

- Sticker paper (the kind you can use in a printer)
- Different flavors of powdered drink mixes
- A small paintbrush
- Scissors
- Markers
- Water

Instructions

1. Sprinkle ¼ teaspoon of powdered drink mix into a ½ teaspoon of water. Use slightly more water and drink mix if you want to make more stickers.

2. Have kids gently brush each sticker with the drink mix solution. Let the stickers dry thoroughly.

3. After the stickers dry, have your child carefully cut out each of the stickers and use markers to decorate them to look like different types of fruit.

4. Scratch, sniff, and stick!

TIPS

- Find stock clip-art images of different kinds of fruit and print them onto the sticker paper. Then paint on the corresponding scent, cut them out, and they're ready to use!

Calming & Alerting Sugar Scrubs

Have you ever used a sugar scrub? At bath and body shops, they can cost a lot of money. Luckily, you can make your very own sugar scrub for much less.

These calming and alerting sugar scrubs are simple and easy to make and are sure to arouse your senses or help you wind down.

Materials

- 1 ½ cups of sugar (brown, organic, or white)
- ¼ cup of oil (olive, coconut, grapeseed, or almond)
- 5-8 drops of essential oils (refer to the reference guide for calming and alerting scents)
- 3 drops of food coloring (optional)
- Mason jar or other airtight container

Instructions

1. Pour all the ingredients into a bowl and mix well until the sugar is completely and evenly distributed.

2. Pour your sugar scrub into a mason jar or other airtight container.

TIPS

- Don't worry too much about the perfect measurements. Experiment with the ingredients until you get the desired texture and scent.

ORAL
ACTIVITIES

Fruity Yogurt Smoothies

Cooking helps children learn functional skills and independence. Smoothies are a great place to start. They are simple to make and fun to taste, which makes them the perfect oral sensory activity.

Ingredients

- 1 Cup milk
- 1 Cup yogurt
- 1 Cup frozen blueberries
- 1 Cup orange juice
- 1 Cup ice
- 1 Tablespoon honey

Materials

- Blender

Instructions

1. Have your kids measure out each ingredient and starting with the milk, pour all the ingredients into the blender.

2. Blend until all the ingredients are mixed together and the ice cubes are as small as they can get.

3. Pour into cups and enjoy.

TIPS

- Encourage your child to suck the smoothie through a straw. Sucking is an organizing sensory activity that is great for increasing focus and attention.

Feather Blowing

Oral sensory activities such as blowing and sucking against resistance can be helpful not only for building strength and oral motor skills but also for contributing to self-regulation, attention, and behavior.

This activity is a fun way to incorporate the oral sensory system into play.

Instructions

1. **Keep It Up:** Just like a game of balloon volleyball, this activity requires lots of coordination and is even more fun with a team. See how long you and your child can keep a feather in the air using only your mouths. You will have to duck, lunge, bob, and race to keep it off the ground.

2. **Obstacle Course:** Set up a simple obstacle course with household items for your child to weave through. Place the feather on the floor and challenge him to get down on his hands and knees (or on his belly) to blow the feather across the floor and around the obstacles.

3. **Feather Hockey:** Set a feather on the kitchen, dining room, or coffee table. Position two players across from each other and see who can be the first to blow the feather off the opposing player's edge of the table.

Ice Boat Races

The object of this sensory play activity is to get an ice cube from one side of a bin to the other but with a catch: you cannot use your hands. You can blow only from the straw.

Materials
– Ice
– Water
– Large plastic bin
– Straws
– Tape

Instructions

1. Mark the container with tape at both ends to make a start and finish line. You can also add a line down the middle of the bin to make lanes for the boats.

2. Fill the container with water and drop in the ice cubes.

3. The kids put their straws in their mouths and blow their ice "boats" from the start line to the finish line.

4. One child can play this game independently by using a timer to try to beat his best time, or you can have two kids race against each other.

Taste Test

For many kids, tastes and textures can have varying effects on alertness, attention, behavior, and arousal levels. For more information, refer to the Oral Sensory Calming and Alerting activities in the *Sensory Resources* section of this book.

Because every child processes oral sensory experiences in their own unique way, it can be helpful to do a little "taste testing" while observing the child's responses to foods that are sweet, sour, chewy, crunchy, and so on. Here's a fun way to experiment with a variety of tastes and textures.

Instructions

1. Set up different tasting stations with small cups or containers of each food or drink.

2. At one station, pour the thick liquid into a cup (or several cups if working with a group) and allow kids to drink it with a straw.

3. For all the stations, give kids a few minutes to try out each food. Observe their reactions and record their likes and dislikes. Does a certain taste, texture, or temperature seem to promote a calmer response? Does another taste, texture, or temperature seem to make the child more alert or active?

Materials

-   Sweet food, such as any sweet candy
-   Sour food, such as a sour gummy bear
-   Salty food, such as potato chips
-   Spicy food, such as peppermint or cinnamon candy
-   Crunchy food, such as carrot sticks, celery sticks, apple slices, or pretzels
-   Chewy food, such as fruit chews, fruit leather, or dried fruit
-   Cold food, such as frozen yogurt, cold water, or ice cubes
-   Hot food, such as broth, soup, or hot chocolate
-   Straws
-   Water
-   Thick liquid, such as a smoothie

TIPS

-   Write a list of your observations and indicate which foods correlated with which types of behavior.

-   Create an "oral sensory box" to keep these foods on hand to use as snacks or sensory breaks throughout the day to promote calm or alert behavior.

Mouthercises

Do you know a kid who makes noises all day, such as blowing raspberries, humming, and/or whistling?

Try some of these fun mouth exercises to give your little one some time and space to get the oral sensory input he needs.

Instructions

Demonstrate each of these sounds and movements for your child or group of children and ask them to imitate. Try these as a warm-up before quiet work sessions or homework, or use as a break during group activities:

1. Buzz like a bee.

2. Make a clicking noise with your tongue.

3. Pucker up and make loud kissing noises.

4. Open your mouth as wide as you can and say "AAAAAHHHHHHH!"

5. Press your lips together as tightly as you can and say "MMMMMMMMMM!"

6. Blow up your cheeks as big as you can like a bubble, then use your hands to "pop" the bubble.

7. Stick your tongue out as far as you can.

8. Have a silly face contest.

TIPS

– Make a visual prompt (such as a picture of a stop sign) or establish a sign (such as holding up one hand and clapping your hands) to show everyone when it is time to stop each noise.

PROPRIOCEPTIVE ACTIVITIES

Bubble Wrap Stomp Art

This recycled art activity presents several opportunities for tactile, vestibular, proprioceptive, and auditory play. You could not pack many more sensory experiences into one activity.

Stomping and jumping on the bubble wrap makes for a full throttle, high-energy painting experience.

Materials

- Washable tempera paint
- Large paper roll
- Various sizes of bubble wrap

Instructions

1. Find a clear space outside and roll out the paper.

2. Squirt paint in drops or lines on the paper.

3. Place the bubble wrap on top of your paint design and let kids jump all over it with bare feet until they cannot jump anymore.

4. Slowly pull off the bubble wrap to see the results.

TIPS

- Be sure to weigh down the paper on the ends with rocks or another heavy object so the wind does not carry it away.

- Try all different sizes of bubble wrap to explore the different effects and sensory experiences.

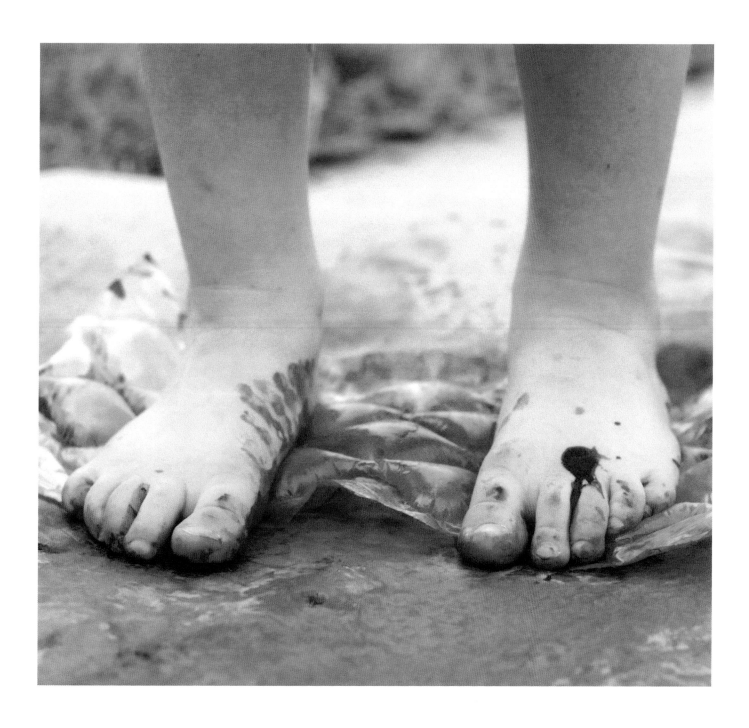

Tire Run Relay

Have you ever seen football players warming up with tire runs? They provide a good workout, and because you have to get your knees up high to avoid tripping over the tires, this exercise also provides excellent proprioceptive input to the lower body as you stomp down into each tire.

Trying this activity with hula hoops provides proprioceptive input and works on body awareness.

Materials

- Hula hoops or sidewalk chalk
- An open space to play

Instructions

Place your hula hoops out on the ground in any pattern you wish for kids to run through.

- Place them in one straight line for kids to jump, hop, or step into.

- Place them in two rows side by side for kids to run through with one foot in each hoop.

- Stagger the hoops a bit so they have to jump or step a little bit further.

- Try a hopscotch pattern with the hula hoops.

TIPS

- If you do not have hula hoops, use sidewalk chalk to draw large circles on the driveway or sidewalk.

- If hula hoops are too big of a challenge, try using circles cut from construction paper or paper plates as the "tires" so the children have less distance to travel between circles.

- Have kids try the course going in a different direction, such as backwards or sideways.

- Set up two hula hoop courses side by side to make it a race for double the fun.

9 Couch Cushion Games

Playing with couch cushions is the ultimate heavy work experience. These big heavy pillows are perfect for lifting, pushing, pulling, jumping on, knocking over, and throwing.

Materials

– Just the cushions from your couch!

TIPS

– Let kids do as much of the lifting, stacking, and arranging of the pillows as possible for an added heavy work bonus.

1. **Follow the Yellow Brick Road:** Help your little ones set up the cushions like a road between two designated points, such as two stools. The kids take turns jumping onto the road and seeing how quickly they can make it from point A to point B without falling off.

2. **Hot Lava:** Have kids help scatter the pillows all around the floor. The ground becomes hot lava, and they have to jump from pillow to pillow to stay safe. For an extra fun challenge: mom or dad becomes the "Lava Dragon," chasing kids around the room.

3. **Wreck It and Fix It:** Kids decide who's going to be the Wrecker and who's going to be the Fixer. They stack all the cushions up as high as they can. The Wrecker takes a running start and knocks the tower over. The Fixer is in charge of stacking the cushions back up. Then switch roles.

4. **Jumpin' Jack:** Lay pillows on the floor so that a section of the floor is covered completely. (Make sure the area is away from furniture or anything else kids could jump into.) Set up a place for kids to jump off (a chair, stool, or ottoman) and watch them jump, leap, and tumble onto the cushions.

5. **King or Queen of the Mountain:** You will need to provide lots of supervision for this one. Help stack the cushions as high as you want (depending on the skill level and age of your child) and spot your little King or Queen as he or she balances on top of the "mountain."

6. **Tunnel Vision:** Work together to prop pillows against each other or onto other furniture to create a tunnel or a bridge for your little ones to crawl through.

7. **Sandwich Shop:** Ingredients: cushions and kids. Stack alternating layers of kids and cushions as high as you can go. Throw a mom or dad in for added fun!

8. **Jailbreak:** Gather the kids together and build a fort around them – four pillows as walls and one or two on top as a roof. You become the guard and they are the "bad guys" trying to break out of jail. Turn your back for a second (or pretend to fall asleep on the job), and your bad guys will break out of their cell. Chase them, recapture them, and repeat.

9. **Pillow Fight:** Just a good old-fashioned pillow fight!

Partner Yoga for Kids

Yoga poses are an excellent way for kids to learn how to move their bodies smoothly and how to grade the force of their movements.

Yoga is challenging, requires focus, and is even more fun with a friend.

Materials

- At least two people
- A timer (if you want a bit of a challenge)

Instructions

1. **Downward Dog Tunnel:** Have the children get on their hands and knees and then lift their hips up to make an upside down "V" with hands and feet on the floor. Can they hold it? Can someone crawl through the tunnel they make with their body?

2. **Boat Pose Footsie:** Have kids sit across from each other with their hands propped behind them. Can they lean their bodies back until their feet hover off the floor and meet in the middle? Can they lift their arms? How long can they hold it?

3. **Double Tree Pose:** Show kids how to stand hip to hip, linking their arms. Gradually, have the children slide their outside leg up so that their foot is resting on the inside of their opposite leg. Can they hold it for a count of 10? Can they straighten their unlinked arms up over their heads?

TIPS

- Incorporate a timer to make it a challenge. Set it when the child begins each pose to see how long they can hold it.

- Try the poses with eyes open and eyes closed.

Homework/Classwork Warm Up

How many times have you started a homework or a classroom assignment only to look around and find a table full of kids who are slumped in their seats, leaning their heads on their hands, and looking like they might fall asleep?

Or maybe you see a different scene – kids who cannot sit still, cannot stop fidgeting with all the pencils and supplies on the table, and cannot seem to slow their bodies down. Either way, this is the activity for you.

Materials

– Pencils

1. **Pencil Rolls:** Give each kid their own pencil. Have them roll the pencil between their hands. Tell them to roll it as fast as they can, then have them roll it slowly. Have one child be the leader and play Red Light, Green Light.

2. **Follow the Leader:** The adult acts as the leader in this game, showing the kids different movements to do with their hands. Rub them together, tap them on legs, tap them on head, clap, snap fingers, or squeeze them together as hard as you can.

3. **Hand Sandwiches:** Place your hand on the table and have a kid put one of his hands on top of yours. Go around the table and have each kid put a hand on top of the pile. Then go around and have everyone place their other hand on top of the pile one at a time.

   Pull your hand out from the bottom of the pile and plop it down (use a little pressure here) on the top of the pile. Whoever's hand is on the bottom will go next, pulling her hand out and patting it onto the top of the pile. Continue like this and see if you can build up speed as you go around the circle.

TIPS

– Many chores can be great proprioceptive warm-up activities as well. We included a list of chores that help calm and focus in the *Sensory Resources* section of this book.

TACTILE ACTIVITIES

Simple Sensory Bins

Sensory bins are an excellent way to encourage tactile play. They are perfect for introducing new textures and exploring new sensations.

Sensory bins are containers filled with some kind of material that kids can feel and manipulate with their hands. The materials can be messy, clean, wet, or dry. Some of our favorite fillers include beans, noodles, and rice. Sensory bins can be adapted to children's individual sensory needs simply by changing the materials inside. A wide variety of materials is available for sensory bins. Refer to the printable guide in the *Sensory Resources* section of this book for some of our favorite options.

Materials
– Sensory bin fillers
– Container
– Scoops, cups, or bowls

Instructions

1. **Choose your container.** This can be as simple as using a store-bought sand table or water table, or you can use one of the following:

   - Bathtub
   - Kitchen sink
   - Paper box lid
   - Shoebox
   - Underbed storage container

   You can also use travel lunch boxes to make bins that are portable or extra large containers for groups of children to play with together.

2. **Choose your filler.** Fill your container with a material that your child will enjoy exploring with their hands. We like to fill the bin's base and leave plenty of room toward the top for exploration.

3. **Choose the Tools.** What you put in the sensory bin will help guide the children in their play. Spoons and bowls will encourage scooping and pouring while tongs and scoops will encourage sorting and comparing.

TIPS

- If your child is hesitant to join in the play, start with dry materials and add only one material at a time. Gradually introduce new textures and encourage your child to slowly explore new sensory experiences.

- Try encouraging the child to play with the sensory bin using a familiar or comforting toy, such as by pushing a train or car through the bin.

Sensory Bags

Sensory bags are the perfect introductory tactile activity for children. They help children to explore their sense of touch without having to get their hands messy.

Sensory bags can be simple and take just minutes to create but provide hours of play.

Materials

- Freezer plastic bags
- Duct tape
- Hair gel
- Baby oil
- Small trinkets such as alphabet beads, sequins, googly eyes, and so on
- Paint

Instructions

Here are three simple and fun sensory bags to try. For all the "recipes" below, place the ingredients in your plastic bag, push all the air out of the bag, then seal the bag with duct tape.

1. **Oil and Water:** Add a few tablespoons of water and baby oil to your freezer bag with a few drops of food coloring of your choice. The oil and water do not mix, which provides a great look and feel.

2. **Discovery Bags:** This is also a simple way to practice visual skills. Fill the bag with rice, flour, or another simple ingredient and add tiny trinkets. You can add items such as alphabet beads, seasonal craft items, themed items, or even small numbers or letters.

3. **Mess-Free Finger Painting:** This is great for children who are hypersensitive to tactile input or for young children who are likely to put finger paint in their mouths. Fill the bag with a few drops of two different colors of paint. Tape the bag to the table on top of a white piece of paper and let your child go to town painting with no mess or fuss..

TIPS

- Always make sure to seal sensory bags properly. Duct tape is a great way to seal the edges.

- If bags begin to look worn or you see any holes starting to form, discard immediately. Close supervision is always recommended.

Simple Sensory Dough Station

Sensory dough presents a variety of textures to children while also boosting hand strength. Sensory doughs can be slimy, crumbly, moldable, smooth, scented, and even edible.

If you are making sensory dough for the first time, be prepared for some experimentation and exploration. Here's how to get started.

Materials

- 1-3 dry ingredients and 1-3 wet ingredients (Refer to the Sensory Dough page in the *Sensory Resources* section of this book.)
- Bowls
- Mixing utensils

Instructions

1. Choose a few ingredients that you think your children will be interested in exploring. We suggest starting with a simple dough such as "cloud dough" or "foam dough." (Refer to the Sensory Dough page in the *Sensory Resources* section of this book for recipes.)

2. Present your children with the ingredients and explain that they can choose two ingredients – one dry and one wet. Generally, it is best to start with equal parts of each ingredient and then experiment from there.
   - Too runny? Add more dry material.
   - Too crumbly? Add a bit more liquid.

3. After you make the perfect consistency, it is time to explore. Children can use these doughs to mold and shape or for the pure enjoyment of tactile input.

TIPS

- In the *Sensory Resources* section of this book, you will find a printable shopping guide for sensory dough ingredients and materials. We included a few simple two-ingredient sensory dough recipes to get you started.

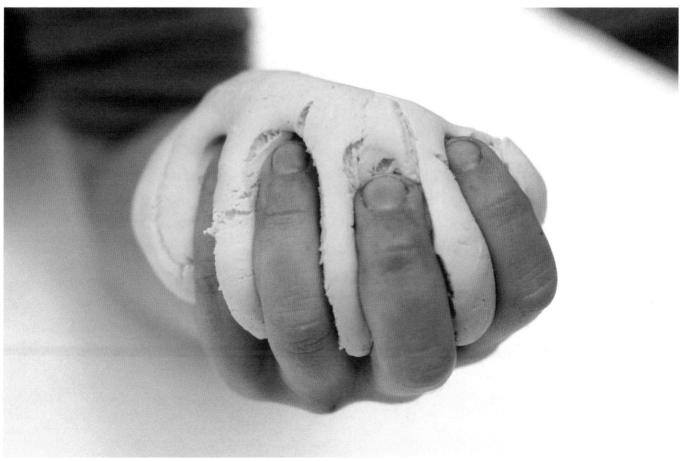

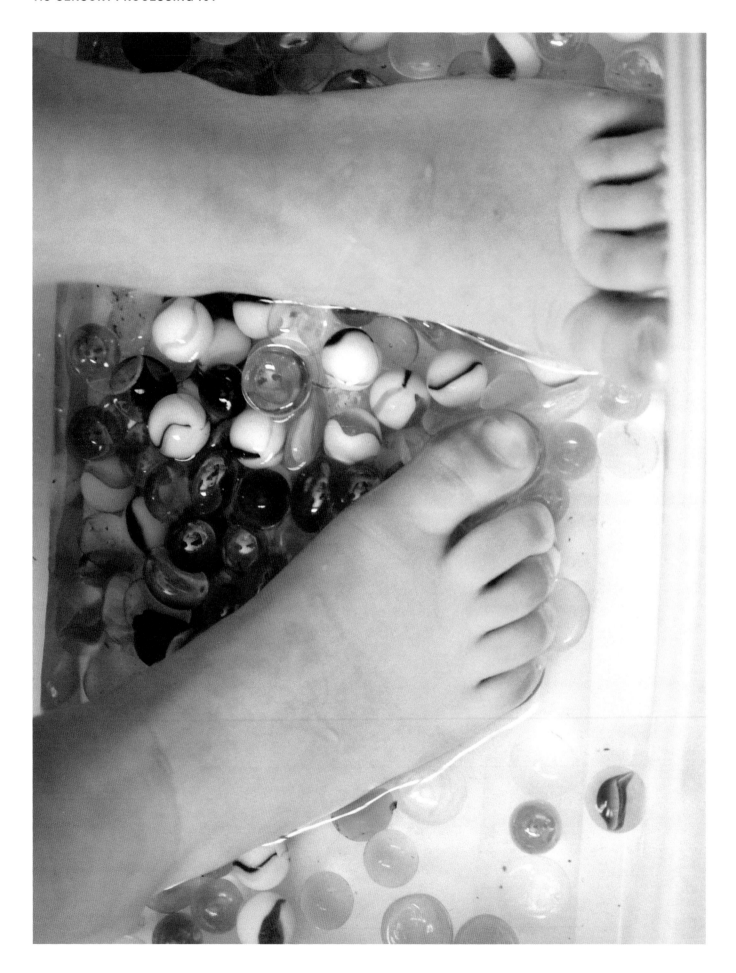

Underwater Pearls

Have your child kick off her shoes and socks and get those toes ready for an underwater adventure. When it comes to tactile play, why should the hands have all the fun?

This is a great "quick on the draw" sensory activity that you can set up using a simple, inexpensive baby pool or even a shallow plastic tub or container.

Materials

- Small pool or shallow tub/container filled halfway with water
- Marbles
- Buckets or other smaller containers (one for each child)

Instructions

1. Spread the marbles all over the bottom of the pool.

2. Have kids sit on chairs or stools just outside the pool, placing their feet into the water.

3. Explain that the marbles are pearls at the bottom of the ocean, and they need to collect the treasures using only their toes.

4. After they practice a little and get the hang of it, have them lift up their feet and drop the "pearls" into a bucket to the side of the pool.

TIPS

- Make it a race to see how many pearls each child can get into their bucket before the timer rings.

- For an added balance challenge, have your child stand beside the pool instead of sitting. They will have to rely on the stability of one leg while the opposite foot works to pick up marbles.

- For an added gross motor challenge, place the collection bucket a little farther away. Can the kids hop on one foot while still keeping the marble safely in their toes until they make it to the bucket?

Touch and Feel Book

Help kids develop the vocabulary to describe tactile experiences by making a book that appeals to the sense of touch.

Children will love reading and touching their book as they learn the meaning of bumpy, smooth, rough, soft, and more.

Instructions

1. Help your child create one page for each tactile description and write the descriptions at the top of the pages.

2. Fasten the pages of the book together by stapling or punching holes and tying with yarn.

3. Place all the sensory materials on the table. One by one, have your child touch an object, describe the object, and gluing it onto the correct page of the book.

Materials

– Cardstock
– Stapler or hole punch
– Yarn
– Craft materials and household items to represent each tactile description. Examples:
   · *Soft*: a feather, craft pompoms, fabric, cotton ball
   · *Smooth*: aluminum foil, wax paper, craft foam
   · *Rough*: sand paper, burlap, twig
   · *Bumpy*: corrugated cardboard, edge of a paper plate
   · *Hard*: piece of plastic, uncooked pasta

TIPS

– Refer back to the book often, using the descriptions and feeling the objects on each page.

– As you read, see if your child can think of other objects that match each description.

VESTIBULAR ACTIVITIES

Swing Activities

For many children, flying through the air on a swing is just about the best entertainment possible. But this activity is also full of amazing sensory benefits. Vestibular input is important for developing balance and helping children feel safe and secure as they explore and play. Swinging is a great way to provide this kind of sensory input for your child.

Instructions

1. **Superman:** Have the child lie with his stomach on the swing and lift arms and legs up as high as possible, flying like Superman.

2. **Tornado:** Have the child sit on the swing. Stand close by and help him turn his swing around and around a few times, then let the tornado spin.

3. **Tug of War:** Have the child lie on the swing on her stomach. Hold one end of a jump rope and give the child the other end to hold with both hands. Stand a few feet away from the swing and gently pull the rope to get her swinging.

4. **Tower Tumble:** Help your child build a tall tower several feet away from the swing using empty cardboard boxes or shoeboxes so that the tower is just out of reach of his feet when he's beginning to swing. Then, see if he can get himself swinging high enough to kick the tower down.

5. **Stand and Swing:** Let your child stand with her feet on the swing holding onto the chains tightly with both hands. If the child is older, encourage her to get herself swinging independently. If you have a younger child, give her a soft push and see if she can keep her balance and continue swinging while standing.

TIPS

- Not all children respond in a positive way to the vestibular input provided by swinging. Start slowly by trying each activity for one minute at a time. Watch the child and how he responds. If he becomes agitated, distressed, sick, or upset during swinging, stop immediately. If you have doubts or concerns about how your child will tolerate swinging, check with an occupational therapist or other medical professional before trying these activities.

Animal Walks

One of the easiest ways to include proprioceptive and vestibular input on a daily basis is with animal walks. Kids love pretending to walk and move like their favorite animals, and it's a fun way to work some proprioceptive and vestibular input into the daily routine.

Instructions

1. **Crab Walk:** Start by squatting down close to the ground. Lean backwards and place your hands on the ground behind you. Now walk sideways, while holding your bottom off the ground and keeping your back straight.

2. **Bear Walk:** Start in the standing position. Bend over and put both hands on the ground. Take a step, moving your right arm and right leg forward at the same time. Then take a step with the left leg and the left arm together. For an additional challenge, try keeping your legs and arms straight.

3. **Frog Jumps:** Start in a squatting position. Place your hands on the floor between your knees. Using your feet, jump forward and land with your hands and feet on the ground, back into a squatting position.

4. **Donkey Kicks:** Start in a standing position. Lean over and put both hands and both feet on the ground. Making sure that the area around you is clear, keep your hands on the ground and jump with your legs kicking behind you.

5. **Turtle Crawl:** Start in a kneeling position, fold forward over your legs and put your elbows on the ground with your palms facing the floor. Keep your bottom on your heels, and keep your elbows and hands on the ground. Reach forward with both hands and scoot your knees forward to meet your hands. Repeat.

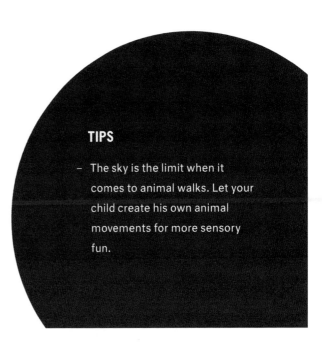

TIPS

- The sky is the limit when it comes to animal walks. Let your child create his own animal movements for more sensory fun.

Sensory Motor Scavenger Hunt

Here's a fun, new twist on a traditional scavenger hunt. Instead of finding or collecting objects, this scavenger hunt will get kids moving, touching, noticing, and interacting with their environment in a completely different way.

Kids will use all their senses in this fun activity. Who will be the first one to find everything on the list?

Materials

– Outdoor Sensory Motor Scavenger Hunt Printable in the *Sensory Resources* section of this book or create your own scavenger hunt list
– Pencils or crayons

Instructions

1. Print or create your scavenger hunt list, round up your little ones, and get started. If you are creating your own scavenger hunt, include items that encourage movement and interaction with materials in the environment rather than just looking for objects. For example: something to balance on, something soft, something to crawl under.

2. Give everyone a pencil or crayon to bring along so they can mark off the things they find. The kids will notice right away that this is not just a typical scavenger hunt.

3. Rather than just finding items on a list, they will have to find the listed objects and perform a variety of movement and sensory tasks.

TIPS

– Use the scavenger hunt inside, then try the same challenges outside. The sensory and movement experiences will be completely different.

– Make it a photo scavenger hunt. Take a picture of your child performing each activity and pictures of each item they find to complete the list.

– Make it a team effort — have two groups competing against each other to find everything on the list.

Row Row Row Your Boat

From the time they're born, kids love to rock and sway. Gentle, repetitive vestibular input is typically calming and organizing to the nervous system.

A few minutes of gentle rocking back and forth is often enough to help a little one regroup and move on if he's feeling overwhelmed. Set sail with these fun and easy activities that provide calming vestibular input.

TIPS

- Sing *Row Row Row Your Boat* or another favorite song as you do each of the activities. Rocking, rolling, or swaying to the rhythm of a familiar song can add to the calming effect.

- Experiment with moving fast and slow. Have the child be the captain of the boat and tell you how to move.

Instructions

1. **Partner Row:** Have two children position themselves in a Tailor Sitting Position (otherwise known as "criss cross applesauce"), facing one another. Tell them to reach out and hold hands and alternately push and pull so their upper bodies rock forward and backward with each motion, like they're rowing a boat.

2. **Rock and Roll:**

   Variation 1: While sitting in the Tailor Sitting position with your child seated in your lap, start rolling backward onto your back. Then using your legs and core, roll back up to sitting again. Repeat this motion, rolling forward and backward like a boat on the waves. This activity has the added benefit of full-body deep pressure input because the child is cuddled on your lap.

   Variation 2: Have kids try it independently. Have the child sit with knees bent and feet on the floor in front of him. Show him how to roll down onto his back and then up to sitting again. Repeat.

3. **Standing Sway:** Stand facing the child holding both of her hands with feet about a foot apart. Slowly extend your arms while the child keeps her body straight and leans backward, then pull the child gently back toward you. Repeat this rowing motion.

DIY Balance Board

You may have seen commercially available balance boards for kids. Several brands are available on the market, and they're helpful for providing children with a vestibular experience while also working on coordination, strengthening, and more.

However, you may have everything you need to make your own. If not, you're only a quick trip to the hardware store and a few dollars away from your own DIY balance board.

Instructions

1. Decorate the board any way you like. You can paint it your child's favorite color, make patterns out of duct tape, or cover it in sticky back felt or other fabric using a hot glue gun.

2. Place the PVC pipe on the floor with the decorated board on top.

3. Hold your child's hands and have him stand on the board with one foot at either end.

4. Help him rock the board from side to side by shifting his weight from one foot to the other.

Materials

- 1 piece of wood (¾ inch thick, 10 inches wide, 2 feet long)
  Note: Wood usually comes in 6-foot pieces, and you can have them cut it to the right lengths for you at the hardware store.

- PVC pipe (1½ inch diameter, 2 feet long)

- Patterned duct tape, paint, colored adhesive-back felt, fabric, or adhesive shelf lining paper

- Hot glue gun (optional)

TIPS

- If your child struggles with keeping her balance, have her start on her knees first for a lower, more steady center of gravity.

- If your child has an easy time with tipping back and forth, see if she can try putting equal weight on both sides of the board to get it to balance perfectly in the middle.

*Warning: This balance board is for use *only* on a carpeted surface and with close supervision by an adult.

VISUAL ACTIVITIES

Mirror, Mirror

This activity taps into kids' visual skills while also working on body awareness, coordination, and social skills.

Instructions

1. Have kids partner up (or an adult can be a partner to a child) and designate one person as the "leader" of each set of partners.

2. Position each set of partners so they are standing face to face.

3. When the leader changes the position of her body (such as lifting an arm or kicking a leg out to the side, the partner has to mimic that position.

4. The leader continues changing positions with her partner imitating every move. Switch partners and repeat.

TIPS

- Position one child in front of a group of children to act as the leader.

- Try playing a speed round where the leader makes position changes rapidly, holding each pose for only a couple of seconds at a time.

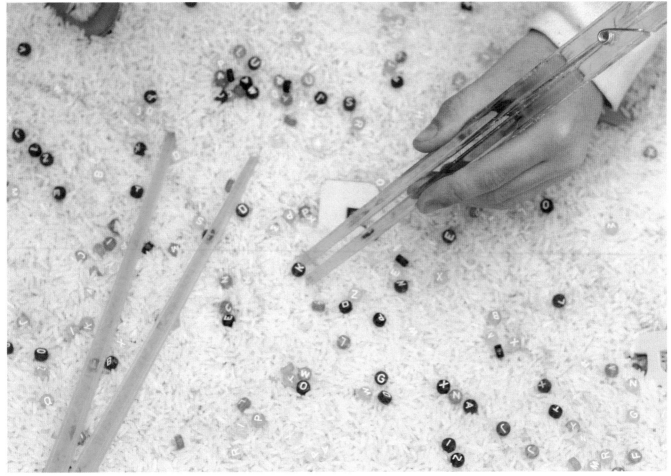

Alphabet Sensory Bin

While sensory bins provide a satisfying tactile play experience for kids, you can also use them to hone in on the other sensory systems. In this activity, you use a sensory bin to get the visual system involved while inspiring learning too.

This activity is a great hands-on learning experience and challenges kids to use their eyes and hands to find a specific object in a competing background.

Materials

- Shoebox-sized (or larger) plastic bin
- Dry alphabet soup pasta (enough to fill your bin about ⅓ of the way)
- Alphabet magnets

Instructions

1. Fill the plastic bin with dry alphabet pasta.

2. Take a handful of alphabet magnets and bury them in the alphabet pasta so they are not visible.

3. Let your child or children go digging for the letters. You have several options for how to play:
    - You name a letter, and the child has to dig until they find the right letter magnet.
    - Kids pull out a letter magnet and have to identify it for you (and/or tell you the letter sound).
    - Write letters all over a blank piece of paper. Kids pull out a letter magnet from the bin and have to match it to the same letter on the paper.
    - Take the letter magnets out of the bin and challenge the kids to try any of the activities above. But this time, they will search for a specific pasta letter instead of the letter magnets.
    - Just let kids explore and play with the bin on their own.

Doodle Guessing Game

This fun game is a cross between an art activity and a sensory activity. It's helpful for developing visual skills, problem-solving strategies, and fine motor skills all at the same time.

Materials

- Pictures from magazines or photographs
- Dry erase markers
- Clear plastic sheet protectors

Instructions

1. Place a picture and clear plastic sheet protector side by side on the table. Tell the child to find specific objects in the picture. For example, if you have a picture of kids playing on a playground, you could ask the child to find the swing, the see-saw, or the slide.

2. Give the child a marker and have him outline or circle on the sheet protector where he thinks the objects would be if the sheet protector were placed on top of the image.

3. Place the plastic sheet on top of the image and see how close the child was. Do the circles match up with the objects?

TIPS

- You can complete this activity with letters, numbers, sight words, or any other concept you might be working on.

- To make it even more challenging, give the child directions for connecting several objects in one picture with a line (like a dot to dot). Then place the sheet protector over the picture and see how close they were to connecting each object.

Sensory Bottles

Sensory bottles, discovery bottles, sensory jars, or calm down jars – whatever you call them, sensory bottles are simply clear containers filled with various materials as a way to encourage visual exploration.

Sensory bottles are helpful tools for babies, toddlers, and children of all ages. You can use them as a calming visual sensory experience or to challenge visual skills in kids.

Materials

– Clear plastic bottles
– Materials to fill the bottles (refer to the printable guide in the Sensory Resources section of this book)

Instructions

Making sensory bottles is simple. Wash a clear plastic bottle, remove the label, and fill with your favorite items to be discovered and explored. Here are two of our favorites:

1. **Galaxy Bottle:** Fill the clear plastic bottle ¼ full with baby oil. Next add water to fill the rest of the bottle. To give your bottle a "galaxy" feel, add two drops of blue food coloring and several drops of red food coloring until you get a color you like. Put the lid on and shake the bottle. The bubbles will almost sparkle, making it look like the bottle is filled with stars.

2. **Look and Find:** In a jar, place small items that match a theme, skill, or concept you are trying to teach, such as letters, numbers, or small toys that are seasonal. Fill the jar with a dry material such as rice or dried beans to cover all the items. You can make a list of objects for children to find in the bottle or just let them search for the objects on their own.

TIPS

– Refer to the printable shopping list of materials in the *Sensory Resources* section of this book to create your own sensory bottles. Test out a variety of objects and materials. You can try a bottle with one material, two materials, or even several. The possibilities are endless.

I Spy With a Twist

Everyone loves "I Spy." It's a classic game for kids, whether you're in a doctor's waiting room, sitting at a table in a restaurant, or in the middle of nowhere on a long road trip.

You can tweak this refreshed version of "I Spy" to target just about any skill.

Instructions

Play "I Spy," but challenge kids to find objects in their surroundings that fit one of the following categories. Each category also lists example questions or statements you can use.

- **Colors:** "How many red things can you spy?"

- **Shapes:** "How many squares can you spy?"

- **Numbers:** "Can you spy five flowers?"

- **Actions:** "I spy something you can throw" or "I spy something you can jump over"

- **Textures:** "I spy something rough" or "I spy something smooth"

- **Alphabet:** "I spy something that starts with the letter "A"

- **Distance:** "I spy something far away" or "I spy something close by"

- **Animal Habitats:** "I spy a place where a bird would live" or "I spy a place where a snake would hide"

- **Memories:** "I spy a place where we camped out one night" or "I spy your favorite place to cuddle up and read a book"

- **Senses:** "I spy something that smells sweet" or "I spy something that makes a loud sound"

TIPS

- Reverse roles. Let your child come up with his own category and *you* find the objects.

- Looking to get more active? Take this game on the move and make it a multisensory experience. For example, if you're using "textures" as a category, run into the yard or around the house and actually touch the different textures that you spy. Or if you're using "actions" as the category, perform the actions with the objects that you spy.

SENSORY
RESOURCES

If you are looking for more information about the sensory systems, Sensory Processing Disorder, ideas for sensory play, and more, you can turn to the following trusted resources.

Top Sensory Websites

Below, you will find a list of seven of our favorite websites about sensory processing and sensory processing disorder. In addition, we have created pages on our websites where you can find more comprehensive and up-to-date lists of websites we recommend including blogs written by pediatric therapists and blogs written by parents who share their journeys of parenting children with sensory needs.

The Inspired Treehouse

http://theinspiredtreehouse.com
Two pediatric therapists, Claire Heffron and Lauren Drobnjak, created this website based on the belief that with a little help, kids can build strong, healthy bodies and minds through play. At The Inspired Treehouse, you'll find an index with hundreds of activities for kids designed to promote healthy gross motor, fine motor, and sensory development. You will also find helpful information about common developmental issues that come up for kids.

Lemon Lime Adventures

http://lemonlimeadventures.com
At this website, parent and former educator Dayna Abraham shares real stories about life's adventures. Turn to this resource for learning ideas, sensory play activities, stories about parenting a child with Sensory Processing Disorder, the everyday trials of parenting, and more.

Project Sensory

http://www.projectsensory.com/
Dayna Abraham and her husband started this company when they discovered they were not the only parents who were ill-equipped to support their child with sensory needs. They believe all children deserve the right tools to support their sensory systems. It is their mission to provide education, support, and awareness of sensory needs through tools, resources, and outreach to classrooms across America.

Sensory Processing Disorder Foundation

http://spdfoundation.net/
This world leader in research, education, and advocacy for Sensory Processing Disorder (SPD) works to improve the lives of children and adults with SPD as well as their families.

SPD Australia

http://www.spdaustralia.com.au
This organization features an extensive online library of resources on Sensory Processing Disorder and is a helpful starting point for learning about sensory processing.

Northshore Pediatric Therapy

http://nspt4kids.com
This team of occupational, physical, speech, and developmental therapists, neuropsychologists, applied behavior analysts, social workers, academic specialists, and dietitians is located in the Chicago area. Their site provides much more than information about their therapy practice. You will find helpful resources, information, and an infographic about Sensory Processing Disorder. Also be sure to check out their Activities to Address Your Child's Tactile Hypersensitivities.

Sensory Processing Disorder

http://sensory-processing-disorder.com
An occupational therapist who has a daughter with SPD created this extensive resource related to Sensory Processing Disorder. This website is a useful place to get information if the world of sensory processing is new to you. Check out the Sensory Processing Disorder Checklist for an overview of sensory behaviors. Read their page about Problem Behaviors in the Classroom and learn some common strategies and accommodations.

Recommended Books

- *The Out of Sync Child* by Carol Kranowitz
- *The Out of Sync Child Has Fun* by Carol Kranowitz
- *Answers to Questions Teachers Ask About Sensory Processing* by Jane Koomar and Carol Kranowitz
- *Understanding Your Child's Sensory Signals* by Angie Voss OTR
- *The Sensory Child Gets Organized* by Carolyn Dalgliesh
- *Sensory Integration: A Guide for Preschool Teachers* by Christie Isbell and Rebecca Isbell
- *The Explosive Child: A New Approach for Understanding and Parenting Easily Frustrated, Chronically Inflexible Children* by Ross W. Greene PhD

Online Support Groups for Parents of Children With Sensory Needs

Support for Sensory Needs
https://www.facebook.com/groups/204754359724169/

Sensory Processing Disorder (SPD) Support
https://www.facebook.com/groups/2217476670/

Project Sensory
http://www.facebook.com/projectsensory

SPD Parent Support
https://www.facebook.com/groups/SPDParentSupport/

SPD Advocacy
https://www.facebook.com/groups/SPDadvocacy/

Alerting and Calming Oral Sensory Activities

Oral sensory input can affect a child's levels of arousal and
potentially even change behaviors by helping a child become more organized
and responsive.

Alerting oral sensory activities can promote awareness and provide the input kids need to focus and attend better at home and at school.

Examples of alerting oral sensory activities include:
- Playing with vibration – battery-powered toothbrush, vibrating toys on cheeks or lips, and so on
- Playing with mouth noises – buzzing like a bee, clicking tongue, humming, or blowing raspberries
- Playing with making faces in a mirror or imitating others' funny faces – opening mouth wide, sticking tongue out, smiling, frowning, or filling cheeks up with air
- Eating crunchy snacks – apples, chips, pretzels, popcorn, raw veggies, toast, graham crackers, or granola
- Eating snacks with sour/sweet tastes – sour gummy worms, grapefruit or orange wedges, or lemonade
- Eating salty snacks – chips, pretzels, or nuts
- Snacking on cold foods – ice chips, popsicles, or frozen grapes
- Trying snacks with intense tastes and temperatures – spicy candies, carbonated beverages, and so on

Calming oral sensory activities can help calm the body so kids can regulate their behavior for learning and other daily tasks.

Examples of calming oral sensory activities include:
- Sucking thicker liquids through a straw – milkshakes, smoothies, applesauce, or pudding
- Drinking from a water bottle with a straw or from an opening that requires sucking
- Resistive chewing, such as chewy toys
- Chewing gum or eating chewy foods – taffy, caramel suckers, gummy bears, licorice, dried fruits, or fruit leathers
- Blowing bubbles, blowing up balloons, or blowing whistles and instruments
- Taking deep breaths in and out slowly
- Singing or humming

Disclaimer: The activities in this book are intended for sensory play and exploration. These activities are not a replacement for therapy to address Sensory Processing Disorder in children. However, some activities may be appropriate for children who have sensory needs with the supervision and recommendation of an occupational therapist. All activities should be facilitated and supervised by an adult. Some of the activities in this book may not be appropriate for children who have allergies or sensitivities to certain sensory materials or foods used for sensory play.

# Alerting and Calming Olfactory Activities

Many children tend to associate strong smells with more alert, focused, and active behavior. Examples of these smells include:
– *Lemon, orange, and other citrus*
– *Peppermint*
– *Coffee*

Softer smells often correspond with calmer, more relaxed behavior for children. Examples of these smells include:
– *Vanilla*
– *Rose*
– *Lavender*

You can incorporate olfactory input into daily exploration and play with your child in several fun ways. Try incorporating the types of scents listed above into the following play ideas:

– **Scented markers**: Have the child color or draw with markers that have calming or alerting scents depending on his needs and preferences.

– **Scented play dough**: Mix extracts or scented oils into a simple homemade play dough recipe.

– **Scented sensory bins**: Add spices, cinnamon sticks, or a few drops of scented oil or extract to a bin full of dried rice or beans.

– **Cooking**: Inviting kids to help in the kitchen gives them exposure to a variety of calming or alerting smells.

– **Scented rice pillow heating pad**: Sew a simple rectangular pouch from sturdy fabric and fill it with dry rice. Add a few drops of scented oil in an alerting or calming scent and heat it for several seconds in the microwave. The warmth will release the scent.

– **Plant a scented garden**: Grow your own alerting and calming scents in your backyard or kitchen. Plant boxes or pots with lavender, rosemary, mint, and other herbs for kids to smell, pick, and explore.

– **Lotions**: Have a couple different scented lotions on hand to use when your child needs an energy boost (peppermint or citrus) or when he needs to calm down (vanilla or lavender).

Sensory Bottles: Quick Reference Guide

LOOSE OBJECTS

- Pipe Cleaners
- Beads
- Foil
- Loom Bands
- Pom-Poms
- Sequins
- Stickers
- Streamers
- Yarn

LIQUID FILLERS

- Hair Gel
- Baby Oil
- Conditioner
- Corn Syrup
- Dish Soap
- Food Coloring
- Glitter Glue
- Vegetable Oil
- Water
- Water Beads

NATURAL OBJECTS

- Corn
- Black Beans
- Flowers
- Leaves
- Lentils
- Pebbles
- Quinoa
- Rice
- Sand
- Sticks

DISCOVERY ITEMS

- Alphabet Stickers
- Colored Items
- Foam Letters
- Foam Numbers
- Googly Eyes
- Letter Beads
- Magnetic Discs
- Marbles
- Number Beads
- Small Toys

Sensory Bins: Quick Reference Guide

NON-FOOD ITEMS

- Beads
- Birdseed
- Buttons
- Cloud Dough
- Coins
- Confetti
- Cotton Balls
- Dirt
- Easter Grass
- Feathers
- Flower Petals
- Grass
- Gravel From Fish Tanks
- Hair Gel
- Hay
- Kinetic Sand
- LEGOs
- Marbles
- Packing Chips
- Paper
- Pom-Poms
- Rocks/Pebbles
- Sand
- Shaving Cream
- Sticks
- Water
- Water Beads
- Yarn

FOOD ITEMS

- Black Beans
- Cereal
- Coconut Oil
- Coffee Beans
- Corn
- Corn Meal
- Edible Water Beads (Tapioca Pearls)
- Flour
- Ice
- Jello
- Lentils
- Oats
- Pasta
- Popcorn Kernels
- Pudding
- Rice
- Salt

MATERIALS TO KEEP ON HAND

- Bowls
- Clothespins
- Cups
- Egg Cartons
- Funnels
- Ice Trays
- Pipe Cleaners
- Scoops
- Spoons
- Tongs
- Tweezers

Disclaimer: The activities in this book are intended for sensory play and exploration. These activities are not a replacement for therapy to address Sensory Processing Disorder in children. However, some activities may be appropriate for children who have sensory needs with the supervision and recommendation of an occupational therapist. All activities should be facilitated and supervised by an adult. Some of the activities in this book may not be appropriate for children who have allergies or sensitivities to certain sensory materials or foods used for sensory play.

Sensory Dough: Quick Reference Guide

DRY INGREDIENTS

- Corn Starch
- Flour
- Powdered Sugar
- Salt
- Sand

WET INGREDIENTS

- Applesauce
- Conditioner
- Frosting
- Jelly
- Marshmallow Creme
- Peanut Butter
- Pumpkin Pie Filling
- Shaving Cream

TOOLS & MANIPULATIVES TO KEEP ON HAND

- Cookie Cutters
- Pipe Cleaners
- Rolling Pins
- Small Items to Hide in Dough (such as beads or marbles)
- Stamps
- Straws
- Toothpicks

SIMPLE FOAM DOUGH

- Shaving Cream + Corn Starch

OTHER COMBINATIONS

- Frosting + Powdered Sugar
- Corn Starch + Conditioner
- Peanut Butter + Powdered Sugar

SIMPLE CLOUD DOUGH

- Flour + Oil

Disclaimer: The activities in this book are intended for sensory play and exploration. These activities are not a replacement for therapy to address Sensory Processing Disorder in children. However, some activities may be appropriate for children who have sensory needs with the supervision and recommendation of an occupational therapist. All activities should be facilitated and supervised by an adult. Some of the activities in this book may not be appropriate for children who have allergies or sensitivities to certain sensory materials or foods used for sensory play.

Sensory Processing Overview

The way the body analyzes and responds to the signals it receives from its environment. Thoughtful, guided exposure to playful sensory experiences ensures that children learn to process and appropriately respond to the sensory stimuli in their environments.

THE AUDITORY SYSTEM

Footsteps, the sound of the wind against your ears, a door creaking, a flushing toilet, even the sounds of someone giving you directions. All these examples have one thing in common: sound.

The auditory sense is how we receive and process the information from the sensory organs inside our ears. When we hear a sound, it travels to our brains to be analyzed so we can generate a response.

THE OLFACTORY SYSTEM

Your favorite piece of chocolate, pancakes on a Saturday morning, rotting fruit in the trash, and your grandma's perfume. All these examples have one thing in common: smell.

The olfactory system is how we pick up information about the odors around us and pass that information along a channel of nerves, where it eventually reaches the brain. Our olfactory systems can discriminate between thousands of different odors and help us recognize whether smells are dangerous, strong, faint, pleasurable, or foul.

ORAL SENSORY PROCESSING

*Biting, chewing, chomping, crunching, sucking, licking, and swallowing. All these activities have two things in common: **taste** and **texture**.*

Oral sensory processing is the way our brains receive input from our mouth and jaw. When we eat or drink, our mouths send information to our brains regarding what we're eating or drinking. This information includes the temperature, texture and taste. Our brains also receive proprioceptive information from the joints of the jaw as we bite and chew.

THE PROPRIOCEPTIVE SYSTEM

*Pushing, pulling, stomping, squeezing, jumping, bending. All these examples have one thing in common: **body position**.*

Proprioception refers to the way our joints and muscles send messages to our brains to provide information about our bodies' positioning and movement. This sense also allows us to grade the force and direction of our movements.

THE VESTIBULAR SYSTEM

*Spinning, turning, flipping, climbing. These sensations all have one thing in common: **movement**.*

The vestibular sense has to do with balance and movement and is centered in the inner ear. When we move our heads, the fluid in the tiny organs of the inner ear moves and shifts, which constantly provides us with information about the position of our heads and bodies in space (*spatial awareness*).

THE TACTILE SYSTEM

*Hugs, clothing, the grass or sand under your feet, the food you eat, the coffee you drink. All these examples have one thing in common: **touch**.*

The tactile sense is how we interpret the information we get from the receptors in our skin. When we feel an object in our environment, our nervous system receives this information and helps us understand and differentiate pressure, temperature, texture, traction, and other tactile qualities of the object. It also lets us determine exactly what it is that we are feeling.

THE VISUAL SYSTEM

*Determining the tint of our shirt to wear for the day, finding our socks in the sock drawer, tracking the teacher as she walks around the room. All these examples have one thing in common: **sight**.*

The visual system is how we receive and process sensory information through our eyes. When we see an object, it is because of the perception of light. Light rays follow a path through the many different structures of our eyes, eventually relaying visual information to the visual cortex in our brains. Here, the brain identifies the object and gives it meaning. We are able to perceive details like color, three-dimensional depth perception, and the location of the object in space.

Sensory Processing Disorder (SPD)

Sometimes children experience difficulty with processing or tolerating one or more types of sensory input. Several possible medical reasons can cause this difficulty, but one of the most common is Sensory Processing Disorder (SPD). For children with SPD, their bodies do not organize and integrate sensory information properly, which makes it difficult for those children to generate appropriate responses to their environments. This can result in a wide range of confusing and sometimes negative behaviors.

Heavy Work Chores for Home or School

HOME

- Switch loads of laundry
- Wipe the counters
- Carry groceries inside
- Load the dishwasher
- Clean the baseboards
- Wash the windows
- Vacuum the carpets
- Mop with a ringer mop
- Sweep with a dust mop
- Take out the garbage

SCHOOL

- Clean dry-erase boards
- Carry copies/books
- Push in chairs
- Water plants
- Return library books
- Carry recess gear
- Sharpen pencils
- Sweep floors
- Empty wastebaskets
- Staple on bulletin board

OUTSIDE

- Rake leaves
- Weed the garden
- Push garbage to the curb
- Stack lawn chairs
- Push a wheelbarrow
- Move rocks with a truck
- Plant flowers in pots
- Gather firewood
- Carry bags of dirt
- Wash outdoor windows

Disclaimer: The activities in this book are intended for sensory play and exploration. These activities are not a replacement for therapy to address Sensory Processing Disorder in children. However, some activities may be appropriate for children who have sensory needs with the supervision and recommendation of an occupational therapist. All activities should be facilitated and supervised by an adult. Some of the activities in this book may not be appropriate for children who have allergies or sensitivities to certain sensory materials or foods used for sensory play.

Sensory Motor Scavenger Hunt

FIND SOMETHING...

☐ To climb

☐ To play catch with

☐ To crawl under

☐ To roll on the ground

☐ To jump over

☐ To walk across

☐ To balance on your head

☐ To use as a drum

☐ Heavy

☐ Rough

☐ Smooth

☐ Soft

☐ Squishy

☐ Hard

Disclaimer: The activities in this book are intended for sensory play and exploration. These activities are not a replacement for therapy to address Sensory Processing Disorder in children. However, some activities may be appropriate for children who have sensory needs with the supervision and recommendation of an occupational therapist. All activities should be facilitated and supervised by an adult. Some of the activities in this book may not be appropriate for children who have allergies or sensitivities to certain sensory materials or foods used for sensory play.

Sensory Processing Red Flag Behaviors Checklist

THE AUDITORY SYSTEM

❏ Exhibits extreme reactions (crying, screaming, running away) or significant difficulty with tolerating sudden noises, specific noises, crowds, and/or loud noises

❏ Startles easily and becomes agitated in noisy environments

❏ Appears distracted by all sounds

❏ Covers ears even at the anticipation of a sound or in uncertain/unfamiliar environments

❏ Has difficulty responding to and following directions presented verbally

❏ Makes constant noises (singing, humming, clicking)

❏ Fails to respond when name is called

❏ Tends to use a loud speaking voice

THE ORAL SENSORY & OLFACTORY SYSTEMS

❏ Seems very reluctant to try new foods or is known as an extremely picky eater

❏ Exhibits extreme resistance to oral sensory experiences like brushing teeth

❏ Refuses to use utensils to eat

❏ Chokes or gags while eating or brushing teeth

❏ Seems to be constantly biting, chewing on, or mouthing hands, clothing, fingers, toys, and other objects

❏ Bites others

❏ Constantly makes mouth noises, such as clicking, buzzing, and/or humming

❏ Stuffs mouth with food at mealtimes

❏ Has difficulty with chewing or drinking from a cup or straw

❏ Displays constant movements of the mouth, such as moving tongue, tapping teeth, and/or rubbing lips

❏ Has strong aversions to certain smells (food or non-food)

❏ Seeks out specific smells regardless of safety (food or non-food)

❏ Frequently smells non-food objects

THE PROPRIOCEPTIVE SYSTEM

❏ Colors/writes with heavy pressure or not enough pressure

❏ Pushes others and/or plays aggressively

❏ Does everything with 100% force, not grading the force of movements adequately

❏ Crashes/falls on the floor constantly throughout the day

❏ Has difficulty with body awareness, such as running into objects or others

❏ Appears tired or sluggish, such as slumping and leaning

THE TACTILE SYSTEM

- Avoids getting hands or face messy
- Avoids activities like finger painting, playing with play dough, and eating messy foods
- Exhibits extreme reactions or tantrums during toothbrushing, bathing, haircuts, and/or dressing
- Has difficulty tolerating certain clothing or textures on skin, such as tags on clothing
- Needs to touch everything and everyone, such as craving hugs and closeness with others, fidgeting with objects, and/or seeking out textures and touch experiences
- Seems unaware when hands or face are messy
- Appears to be unaware of pain
- Avoids touch, hugs, or other physical contact

THE VESTIBULAR SYSTEM

- Seems to be constantly moving, fidgeting, and/or spinning around
- Appears fearful of movement such as stairs, playground equipment, and/or swings
- Appears uncoordinated or clumsy, such as bumping into things, falling, and having difficulty learning new motor tasks
- Slumps, slouches, or leans on desk or on walls when walking in the hallway
- Has difficulty with maintaining balance when walking and during gross motor play
- Has difficulty with visual activities such as focus or tracking

THE VISUAL SYSTEM

- Seems easily distracted by surrounding visual stimuli, such as posters or art on the walls as well as activity in the room.
- Has difficulty visually focusing on a task like coloring a picture or completing a worksheet
- Fails to notice surroundings unless others point them out
- Stares intently at objects or becomes fixated on visual stimuli, such as fans or lights
- Arranges objects in a specific way repeatedly, such as lining objects up or stacking objects

Auditory Sensory Cheat Sheet

AUDITORY AVOIDING BEHAVIORS

- Cries, screams, or becomes angry at sudden noises
- Has strong emotions when noise volume increases
- Covers ears or hides in social situations
- Avoids everyday noises such as toilet flushing or water flowing
- Seems bothered by high-pitched noises such as whistles, chalk, and violins
- Appears distressed by metallic sounds such as silverware clinking or noises from a xylophone

AUDITORY SEEKING BEHAVIORS

- Prefers loud music
- Seems to always use an "outside voice"
- Puts musical instruments right next to the ears
- Makes loud noises in quiet settings
- Enjoys loud noises
- Craves common noises such as an air conditioner, a fan, or water running
- Seems to be calmed by noises or certain music

QUICK AND SIMPLE AUDITORY ACTIVITIES

- Matching sound games
- Activities that connect movement with sounds
- Rhymes and chants
- Noise-reducing earmuffs
- Calming music

- Quiet room or space to retreat
- Sound machines
- Musical instruments
- Pre-recorded books
- Earplugs

Olfactory Sensory Cheat Sheet

OLFACTORY AVOIDING BEHAVIORS

- Avoids particular smells
- Becomes agitated or frustrated around certain smells
- Tends to resort to fight or flight methods when encountering certain smells
- Gags with certain smells or foods
- Avoids familiar foods due to smells
- Indicates that foods do not taste appealing
- Tells other people they smell bad
- Avoids public places
- Dislikes being hugged or being close to other people

OLFACTORY SEEKING BEHAVIORS

- Smells objects that seem odd
- Enjoys strong scents
- Prefers foods with strong smells
- Fails to notice dangerous smells
- Tends to eat or drink dangerous items due to inability to smell "danger"
- Exhibits trouble identifying smells of foods
- Smells objects constantly
- Smells people constantly

QUICK & SIMPLE OLFACTORY ACTIVITIES

- Aromatherapy
- Scented fidget toys
- Lavender scents
- Scented rice play
- Sweet and sour sorting
- Blindfold smells
- Scented playdough
- Scent matching
- Guess that scent
- Taste and smell games
- Berry smoothies
- Scented finger painting

Oral Sensory Cheat Sheet

ORAL AVOIDING BEHAVIORS

- Avoids certain textures of foods
- Exhibits difficulty when trying new foods
- Gags, chokes, or drools often
- Exhibits difficulty using a straw
- Experiences problems with chewing or swallowing
- Avoids mushy foods

ORAL SEEKING BEHAVIORS

- Craves certain foods
- Prefers spicy or hot foods
- Bites frequently
- Bites and/or chews nails
- Mouths non-food items
- Chews furniture, toys, pencils, and so on

QUICK & SIMPLE ORAL MOTOR ACTIVITIES

- Blow bubbles
- Blow whistles and other instruments
- Play taste guessing games
- Try one new food before dinner
- Make an edible necklace

- Chew gum or hard candy
- Drink from a water bottle with a bite valve
- Eat applesauce through a straw
- Use alternative chewy toys

Proprioceptive Sensory Cheat Sheet

PROPRIOCEPTIVE AVOIDING BEHAVIORS

- Appears lazy or lethargic
- Avoids active activities, such as running, jumping, or climbing
- Is a picky eater
- Prefers to sit still
- Avoids touch from others
- Seems uncoordinated
- Seeks familiar activities
- Exhibits difficulty using stairs

PROPRIOCEPTIVE SEEKING BEHAVIORS

- Runs into objects, walls, or people
- Uses extreme force
- Stomps or walks loudly
- Kicks, bites, and/or hits
- Invades personal space
- Chews clothing, pencils, or fingers

QUICK & SIMPLE PROPRIOCEPTIVE ACTIVITIES

- Trampolines
- Wall pushups
- Yoga stretches
- Playdough
- Gardening

- Bear hugs
- Massages
- Animal walks
- Carrying and/or lifting boxes
- Chores

Tactile Sensory Cheat Sheet

TACTILE AVOIDING BEHAVIORS

- Avoids certain textures or clothing
- Avoids or dislikes messy play
- Exhibits distress with certain clothing such as tight pants, seams in socks, and new textures
- Is extremely ticklish
- Dislikes getting face and hands washed
- Avoids hugs or physical contact
- Acts fearful of large crowds
- Acts anxious or over-excited over light touch
- Dislikes hair brushing, washing, or drying
- Is a picky eater
- Walks only on toes
- Refuses to walk barefoot

TACTILE SEEKING BEHAVIORS

- Prefers tight clothing
- Always seems dirty or messy
- Seems unaware of being touched by others
- Exhibits a high pain tolerance
- Has low impulse control and seems to touch everything
- Craves vibrations
- Plays aggressively with other children, such as hitting, pushing, and pinching
- Constantly touches things around them
- Constantly mouths objects

QUICK & SIMPLE TACTILE ACTIVITIES

- Tight squeezes: Deep pressure massage, hand squeezes, and so on
- Squish box: Surrounded by pillows
- Weighted activities: Vests, blankets, and so on
- Sensory bins filled with rice, flour, and so on
- Sensory doughs such as playdough, cloud dough, moon sand, and so on
- Finger painting

Vestibular Sensory Cheat Sheet

VESTIBULAR AVOIDING BEHAVIORS

- Acts scared of movement activities
- Seems fearful around playground equipment, such as stairs, swings, merry-go rounds, and so on
- Seems fearful of elevators
- Dislikes being turned upside down or being picked up
- Tends to appear clumsy or uncoordinated
- Tends to appear stubborn
- Avoids stairs or holds onto the railing tightly with both hands

VESTIBULAR SEEKING BEHAVIORS

- Seems unable to sit still
- Needs to be in constant motion, such as fidgeting, rocking, swinging, or spinning
- Seems very impulsive
- Seems unable to get enough movement
- Runs everywhere instead of walking
- Takes unsafe risks both inside and outside
- Prefers to be upside down or hangs off a couch or chair

QUICK & SIMPLE VESTIBULAR ACTIVITIES

- Freeze dancing
- Spinning
- Hanging upside down

- Riding on trikes and bikes
- Jumping on trampolines
- Swinging

Visual Sensory Cheat Sheet

VISUAL AVOIDING BEHAVIORS

- Covers eyes, squints, or screens out sights
- Avoids bright lights and/or sunlight
- Withdraws from participating in group movement
- Scared of moving objects
- Avoids direct eye contact
- Experiences frequent headaches, dizziness, or nausea when using sight
- Seems unaware of contrasting colors and/or tones
- Seems clumsy due to being unaware of objects in a path
- Seems unable to determine distance
- Rubs eyes

VISUAL SEEKING BEHAVIORS

- Stares at bright lights, flickers, or direct sunlight
- Stares at moving objects
- Moves and shakes head during writing or fine motor activities
- Holds items close for inspection
- Seems unaware of new people/items in an environment
- Exhibits difficulty focusing on stationary objects
- Frequently loses the place on a page
- Seeks visual stimulation such as spinning, patterns, fans, and fences

QUICK & SIMPLE VISUAL ACTIVITIES

- Flashlight tag
- Light table activities
- Sensory bottles
- Activities involving drawing, painting, and gluing
- Alphabet I Spy
- Marble mazes
- Labyrinths

- Visual schedules
- Activities to reduce clutter
- Eye breaks
- Sensory retreats
- Color matching games
- Guesstimation jars
- Bean bag toss

Index by Behavior

Clothing, distressed by certain 32-37	
Clothing, prefers tight 26-30, 32-37	
Clumsy 26-30, 32-37, 38-41	
Clumsy due to being unaware of objects in a path 38-41, 42-46	
Colors, unaware of contrasting 42-46	
Common noises, craves 8-13	
Constantly touches things around them 26-30, 32-37	
Covers ears 8-13	
Covers eyes, squints, or screens out sights 42-46	
Crashes into things 26-30	
Craves certain foods 14-19, 20-25	
Craves common noises such as an air conditioner, a fan, or water running 8-13	
Craves vibrations 8-13, 26-30, 32-37	
Cries, screams or becomes angry at sudden noises 8-13	
Crowds, fearful of large 8-13, 14-19, 32-37, 38-41, 42-46	
Dangerous smells, doesn't notice 14-19	
Dangerous things, eats or drinks 20-25	
Dangerous things, smells 14-19	
Difficulty tolerating new foods 14-19, 20-25, 32-37	
Difficulty using a straw 20-25	

Direct eye contact, avoids 42-46	
Direct sunlight, stares at 42-46	
Dirty, always seems 32-37	
Dirty, not aware of being 32-37	
Dislikes being turned upside down or picked up 38-41	
Dislikes getting face and hands washed 32-37	
Dislikes hair brushing, washing or drying 32-37	
Dislikes messy play 32-37	
Dislikes transitions 8-13, 32-37, 38-41, 42-46	
Disruptive in loud places 8-13	
Distance, unable to determine 38-41, 42-46	
Distracted easily 8-13, 26-30, 32-37, 38-41, 42-46	
Distressed by certain clothing such as tight pants, seams in socks, and new textures 32-37	
Distressed by loud sounds 8-13	
Distressed by metallic sounds such as silverware clinking or noises from a xylophone 8-13	
Dizziness, frequent 38-41, 42-46	
Doesn't notice dangerous smells 14-19	
Drinks dangerous things due to seeking out strong or specific tastes 20-25	
Drools often 20-25	

Ears, covering
8-13

Easily distracted
8-13, 26-30, 32-37, 38-41, 42-46

Eating, problems with
20-25

Eats dangerous things due to seeking out strong or specific tastes
20-25

Elevators, fearful
8-13, 38-41

Enjoys loud noises
8-13

Enjoys strong scents
14-19

Everyday noises, avoids
8-13

Extreme force during movement activities, uses
26-30, 32-37

Extremely ticklish
32-37

Eye contact, avoids direct
42-46

Eyes, cover
42-46

Eyes, holds objects close to
42-46

Eyes, rubs
42-46

Face washed, dislikes having
32-37

Fearful around playground equipment such as stairs, swings, merry-go rounds, etc
38-41, 42-46

Fearful of elevators
8-13, 38-41

Fearful of large crowds
8-13, 14-19, 32-37, 38-41, 42-46

Fidgets frequently
26-30, 32-37, 38-41, 42-46

Fight or flight methods, resorts to
8-13, 14-19, 20-25, 32-37, 38-41, 42-46

Fingernails, bites or chews
20-25, 26-30

Flickers, stares at
42-46

Foods with strong smells, prefers
14-19

Foods, avoids certain textures of
20-25, 32-37

Foods, avoids due to smell of certain
14-19

Foods, craves certain
14-19, 20-25

Foods, difficulty tolerating new
14-19, 20-25, 32-37

Foods, gags with certain
14-19, 20-25

Foods, prefers spicy or hot
14-19, 20-25

Foods, trouble identifying smells of
14-19

Frequent biting
20-25, 26-30

Frequent headaches, dizziness or nausea during movement
38-41, 42-46

Frequent headaches, dizziness or nausea during visual activities
38-41, 42-46

Frequently loses the place on a page when reading or working
42-46

Frustrated around certain smells
14-19

Gags often
20-25

Gags with certain smells or foods
14-19, 20-25

Group movement activities, withdraws from
8-13, 32-37, 38-41, 42-46

Hair brushing, washing or drying, dislikes
32-37

Hands washed, dislikes having
32-37

Hangs off couch or chair 38-41, 42-46	
Has difficulty ascending or descending stairs 26-30, 38-41, 42-46	
Headaches, frequent 38-41, 42-46	
High pain tolerance 32-37	
High pitched noise, bothered by 8-13	
Hits self and others 26-30, 32-37	
Holds objects close to eyes 42-46	
Holds on to a stair railing tightly with both hands 26-30, 38-41	
Hot and spicy foods, prefers 14-19, 20-25	
Hugs, avoids 26-30, 32-37	
Impulsive, can be very 8-13, 26-30, 32-37, 38-41	
Invades others' personal space 14-19, 26-30, 32-37	
Jumping, avoids 26-30, 32-37, 38-41	
Kicks people or things 26-30, 32-37	
Large crowds, fearful 8-13, 14-19, 32-37, 38-41, 42-46	
Lazy or lethargic 26-30, 32-37, 38-41	
Loud music or noises, prefers 8-13	
Loud noises, distressed at 8-13	
Loud places, disruptive in 8-13	
Makes loud noises in quiet settings 8-13	
Melts down easily 8-13, 14-19, 20-25, 32-37, 38-41, 42-46	
Messy play, avoids or dislikes 32-37	
Messy, always seems 32-37	
Messy, not aware of being 32-37	
Metallic sounds, distressed by 8-13	
Mouths non-food items and objects 20-25, 32-37	
Movement activities, scared of 8-13, 32-37, 38-41	
Movement activities, uses extreme force during 26-30, 32-37	
Movement activities, withdraws from group 8-13, 32-37, 38-41, 42-46	
Movement, seeks out (fidgets, rocks, swings, spins) 26-30, 32-37, 38-41	
Moves and shakes head during writing or fine motor activities 38-41, 42-46	
Moving objects, scared of 8-13, 32-37, 42-46	
Moving objects, stares at 42-46	
Music, calmed by certain 8-13	
Music, prefers loud 8-13	
Nails, bites or chews 20-25, 26-30	
Nausea, frequent 38-41, 42-46	
New foods, difficulty tolerating 14-19, 20-25, 32-37	
New people/items, seems unaware of 42-46	
Noises, bothered by high pitch 8-13	
Noises, calmed by certain 8-13	

Noises, craves common 8-13	Prefers tight clothing 26-30, 32-37
Noises, cries or is angry at sudden 8-13	Prefers to be upside down or hangs off a couch or chair 38-41, 42-46
Noises, enjoys loud 8-13	Prefers to sit still 8-13, 26-30, 32-37, 38-41, 42-46
Noises, makes loud 8-13	Problems chewing, swallowing, or eating 20-25
Non-food items, chews 20-25, 26-30	Public places, avoids 8-13, 14-19, 32-37, 42-46
Non-food items, mouths 20-25	Pushes people or things 26-30, 32-37
Not aware of being dirty or messy 32-37	Quiet settings, makes loud noises in 8-13
Not aware of being touched by others 32-37	Refuses to go barefoot 32-37
Objects, mouths 20-25, 32-37	Resorts to fight or flight methods 8-13, 14-19, 20-25, 32-37, 38-41, 42-46
Outside voice, always uses 8-13	Risks, takes unsafe 26-30, 38-41
Overly excited by light touch 32-37	Rocks, constantly 38-41
Page, frequently loses the place on a 42-46	Rubs eyes 42-46
Pain tolerance, high 32-37	Running, avoids 26-30, 32-37, 38-41
People, smells other 14-19	Runs everywhere, instead of walking 26-30, 38-41
Personal space, invades others' 14-19, 26-30, 32-37	Runs into objects, walls, or people 26-30, 38-41, 42-46
Physical contact, avoids 26-30, 32-37	Scared of movement activities 8-13, 32-37, 38-41
Picked up, dislikes being 38-41	Scared of moving objects 8-13, 32-37, 42-46
Picky eater 14-19, 20-25, 32-37	Seeks out movement (fidgets, rocks, swings, spins) 26-30, 32-37, 38-41
Playground equipment, fearful 38-41, 42-46	Seeks out strong or specific tastes 20-25
Prefers foods with strong smells 14-19	Seeks visual stimulation such as spinning, patterns, fans and fences 42-46
Prefers loud music 8-13	
Prefers spicy or hot foods 14-19, 20-25	

Ticklish, extremely 32-37	
Tight clothing, prefers 26-30, 32-37	
Toes, walk on 26-30, 32-37, 38-41	
Toilet flushing, avoids noise of 8-13	
Tones, unaware of contrasting color 42-46	
Touch, made anxious by 32-37	
Touch, avoids 26-30, 32-37	
Touch, overly excited by 32-37	
Touched by others, not aware of being 32-37	
Touches things, constantly 26-30, 32-37	
Transitions, dislikes 8-13, 32-37, 38-41, 42-46	
Trouble identifying smells of foods 14-19	
Unable to determine distance 38-41, 42-46	
Unable to sit still 8-13, 26-30, 32-37, 38-41	
Unaware of contrasting colors or tones 42-46	
Unaware of new people or items 42-46	
Unaware of objects in path, seems clumsy 38-41, 42-46	
Uncoordinated 26-30, 32-37, 38-41, 42-46	
Upside down, dislikes being 38-41	
Upside down, prefers being 38-41, 42-46	
Uses extreme force during movement activities 26-30, 32-37	
Vibrations, craves 8-13, 26-30, 32-37	
Violins, bothered by sound of 8-13	
Visual stimulation, seeks 42-46	
Walks loudly 8-13, 26-30, 32-37	
Walks on toes 26-30, 32-37, 38-41	
Water flowing, avoids noise 8-13	
Whistles, bothered by 8-13	
Withdraws from participating in group movement activities 8-13, 32-37, 38-41, 42-46	

Index

About the Authors

Dayna Abraham is a National Board Certified early childhood teacher turned homeschooling mom of three. She started blogging at Lemon Lime Adventures to share her real-life experiences with homeschooling and supporting her son with Sensory Processing Disorder as well as to share life's sweet and sour moments. Her mission is to remain down to earth while providing ideas for intentional learning experiences ranging from science to sensory play. Visit Lemon Lime Adventures at http://lemonlimeadventures.com/

Claire Heffron and Lauren Drobnjak are practicing pediatric occupational and physical therapists who blog at The Inspired Treehouse. Pam Braley, also an occupational therapist, is a co-creator and contributor to The Inspired Treehouse. Claire holds a Master of Science in Occupational Therapy from The University of North Carolina and has been practicing in public and specialized school-based settings for 10 years. Lauren graduated from Youngstown State University with a Bachelor's of Science in Physical Therapy. She has practiced for more than 15 years in both clinical and school-based settings. Pam holds a Bachelor's of Science degree in Occupational Therapy from The Ohio State University and has 18 years experience practicing in pediatric clinical and school-based settings. Claire, Lauren, and Pam use outcome- and evidence-based techniques to evaluate and treat children with a wide range of diagnoses and developmental delays. The three therapists also share a passion for promoting healthy development for all children by providing information, activities for kids, and resources at The Inspired Treehouse. Visit The Inspired Treehouse at *http://theinspiredtreehouse.com/*